The Early Modern Englishwoman:
A Facsimile Library of Essential Works

Series I

Printed Writings, 1500–1640: Part 2

Volume 9

Jane Owen

Advisory Board:

Margaret J.M. Ezell
Texas A & M University

Elaine Hobby
Loughborough University

Suzanne W. Hull
The Huntington Library

Barbara K. Lewalski
Harvard University

Stephen Orgel
Stanford University

Ellen Rosand
Yale University

Mary Beth Rose
University of Illinois, Chicago

Hilda L. Smith
University of Cincinnati

Retha M. Warnicke
Arizona State University

Georgianna Ziegler
The Folger Shakespeare Library

The Early Modern Englishwoman: A Facsimile Library of Essential Works

Series I

Printed Writings, 1500–1640: Part 2

Volume 9

Jane Owen

Introduced by
Dorothy L. Latz

General Editors
Betty S. Travitsky and Patrick Cullen

Ashgate

Aldershot • Burlington USA • Singapore • Sydney

The Introductory Note copyright © Dorothy L. Latz 2000

All rights reserved. No part of this publication may be reproduced, stored in a retrieval system, or transmitted in any form or by any means, electronic, mechanical, photocopying, recording, or otherwise without the prior permission of the publisher.

Published by
Ashgate Publishing Ltd
Gower House
Croft Road
Aldershot
Hants GU11 3HR
England

Ashgate Publishing Company
131 Main Street
Burlington
Vermont 05401
USA

Ashgate website: http://www.ashgate.com

British Library Cataloguing-in-Publication Data
Owen, Jane
   The early modern Englishwoman : a facsimile library of
essential works.
   Part 2: Printed writings, 1500–1640: Vol. 9
   1. English literature – Early modern, 1500–1700   2. English
literature – Women authors   3. Women – England – History –
Renaissance, 1450–1600 – Sources   4. Women – England –
History – Modern period, 1600– – Sources   5. Women – Literary
collections
   I. Title   II. Travitsky, Betty S.   III. Cullen, Patrick Colborn,
   1940–   IV. Latz, Dorothy L.   V. An antidote against purgatory
   820.8'09287

Library of Congress Cataloging-in-Publication Data
The early modern Englishwoman: a facsimile library of essential works. Part 2. Printed writings, 1500–1640 / general editors, Betty S. Travitsky and Patrick Cullen.

See page vi for complete CIP Block 99-56944

The woodcut reproduced on the title page and on the case is from the title page of Margaret Roper's trans. of [Desiderius Erasmus] *A Devout Treatise upon the Pater Noster* (circa 1524).

ISBN 1 84014 222 7

Printed in Great Britain by Antony Rowe Ltd, Chippenham, Wiltshire

CONTENTS

Preface by the General Editors

Introductory Note

An Antidote Against Purgatory

Library of Congress Cataloging-in-Publication Data
Owen, Jane, of God-stow.
 [Antidote against purgatory]
 Jane Owen/introduced by Dorothy L. Latz.
   p.   cm. – (The early modern Englishwoman. Printed writings, 1500–1640, Part 2: v. 9)
 Originally published: An antidote against purgatory, St. Omer, 1635.
 ISBN 1–84014–222–7
   1. Spiritual life–Catholic Church–Early works to 1800.   2. Purgatory–Early works to 1800.   I. Latz, Dorothy L.   II. Title.   III. Series.

BX2350.2.O98 2000
274.2'06–dc21

99–56944

PREFACE
BY THE GENERAL EDITORS

Until very recently, scholars of the early modern period have assumed that there were no Judith Shakespeares in early modern England. Much of the energy of the current generation of scholars has been devoted to constructing a history of early modern England that takes into account what women actually wrote, what women actually read, and what women actually did. In so doing the masculinist representation of early modern women, both in their own time and ours, is deconstructed. The study of early modern women has thus become one of the most important—indeed perhaps the most important—means for the rewriting of early modern history.

The Early Modern Englishwoman: A Facsimile Library of Essential Works is one of the developments of this energetic reappraisal of the period. As the names on our advisory board and our list of editors testify, it has been the beneficiary of scholarship in the field, and we hope it will also be an essential part of that scholarship's continuing momentum.

The Early Modern Englishwoman is designed to make available a comprehensive and focused collection of writings in English from 1500 to 1750, both by women and for and about them. The first series, *Printed Writings, 1500–1640*, provides a comprehensive if not entirely complete collection of the separately published writings by women. In reprinting these writings we intend to remedy one of the major obstacles to the advancement of feminist criticism of the early modern period, namely the unavailability of the very texts upon which the field is based. The volumes in the facsimile library reproduce carefully chosen copies of these texts, incorporating significant variants (usually in appendices). Each text is preceded by a short introduction providing an overview of the life and work of a writer along with a survey of important scholarship. These works, we strongly believe, deserve a large readership—of historians, literary critics, feminist critics, and non-specialist readers.

The Early Modern Englishwoman will also include separate facsimile series of *Essential Works for the Study of Early Modern Women* and of *Manuscript Writings*. It is complemented by *Women and Gender in Early Modern England, 1500–1750*, a series of original monographs on early modern gender studies, also under our general editorship.

New York City
2000

INTRODUCTORY NOTE

Few facts are known about Catholic recusant Jane Owen. The title page of *An Antidote Against Purgatory*, her only known work, tells us that in 1634 when this volume was published at St Omer (then in Spanish-held Flanders), Jane was already deceased, but she was necessarily still living after 1617 when the treatise of Bellarmine which she here partially translates, *De Gemitu Columbae* ... , was first published in Latin in Rome. She would still be living in 1625, date of the accession of King Charles I to the English throne, as her request for prayers for that king would indicate (190; 192). Although it is possible that Jane Owen lived in exile on the Continent (willingly or otherwise), her mature, concrete and intimate descriptions of the lives and family circumstances of the Catholics in England would seem to indicate that she had remained there most of her life (152–56; 181–85; 218–226; quotations below). Her knowledge of the lives of English Catholics who had fled to the Continent to practise their faith, however, seems to have been based on her personal experiences. She may have been one of those recusants who passed back and forth across the Channel surreptitiously to collect alms for the poverty-stricken English recusant colleges, seminaries, schools and convents abroad, for which she here urges donations from the recusants in England unaware of the hardships of the exiles. She seems to remind her readers – who already seem to be acquaintances – that she has no children (111–12).

Much is known about Jane Owen's relatives, which may assist us in picturing her circumstances. The title page informs us that she is of 'Godstow in Oxfordshire', one of the estates which was first bestowed on George Owen (d. 1558) for his services as physician to Henry VIII, Edward VI and Queen Mary Tudor, and which was then handed down to his descendants (Lee), who in Jane's lifetime were well-known Catholic recusants both at Godstow and on the Continent (Lee; Cooper; Gillow; Hamilton). George Owen's eldest son, Richard, had married

Mary Chamberlain, daughter of Sir Leonard Chamberlain of Sherburne Castle, and by 1615 Richard's grandson John Owen, a resident of Godstow, was imprisoned for Catholic recusancy and then permanently exiled to Spain (Lee). Mary Chamberlain Owen's brother also had been exiled to the Low Countries where he had married, and later his son was appointed Bishop of Ypres in 1626 (Cooper; Gillow; Hamilton). Among their other relations one also finds Abbess Neville of the recusant English Benedictines of Pontoise (Hamilton).

Was Jane Owen one of the hidden members of Mary Ward's proposed new 'Institute', as it was called? We know that in Jane's lifetime England's Mary Ward had established schools in Flanders for recusant English girls, and had received tentative permission from Rome to proceed with her plan for a religious order to keep the Catholic faith alive in England. Her plan necessarily entailed a lack of external identification and secrecy concerning membership, especially in England because of the penal laws (Guilday, Chapter VI, and Chambers cited therein). We also know that at this time Mary Ward had hidden members of her budding 'Institute' living within their family circles in England, while striving and succeeding against civil law to send girls to religious schools and young men to seminaries and colleges on the Continent (Guilday), practices which Jane here encourages. Jane also refers to her own preaching: ' … let a woman once preach to women', she says (186), while exhorting her compatriots to give alms. This is a courageous initiative, for in Jane's time Mary Ward's followers were criticized at Rome by the English Diocesan clergy for publicly preaching, an activity forbidden to women (Guilday and Chambers cited therein).

Jane's personal exhortations and descriptions of family and social conditions in England give us unique glimpses of social history written by a recusant woman in the first person: men waste their money in 'gallantry of apparell', 'running-horses', 'dyce', and 'wasteful Christmasses' (152); women waste money on expensive gowns with frequent new ones, as well as on jewellery and on games such as 'Gleeke' (181); idle young men borrow from their elder brothers (219–20), frequent alehouses, and often become 'Fathers before they be Husbands' (220); young women often end in miserable marriages because of their indiscretions (223–24).

Jane Owen writes in simple, explanatory prose, but she uses vivid metaphors and symbols customary for her era. She compares herself to a 'skillfull physition, who can extract medicinable and healthfull physick, out of hurtfull and venomous ... hearbs' (275). She urges leaving the 'Stage or Theater of this world ... for the gayning of that Celestiall Kingdome; in compare of which, all the kingdomes upon the Earth deserve not to be Types or adumbrations' (193). Her thoughts, however, reflect several of Bellarmine's ideas which were considered new and debatable among his fellow ecclesiastics at the Vatican in that era, such as his teaching that it is the duty of the wealthy to help the poor, a concept Jane often repeats, although the idea would be far from 'novel' today.

We are told on the title page that Jane Owen was a 'learned lady', as one may see by her linguistic skills and translations. However, Jane seems unaware of some post-Council of Trent trends on the Continent in her times. This may indicate that for most of her life she had lived in England, where Catholic instruction/preaching was forbidden by the penal laws. For example, Jane repeatedly depicts purgatory as a place of torture, with descriptions influenced by the fanciful imagery of medieval legends and superstitions specifically criticized by the Council of Trent as lacking theological substance, and the Council issued an edict stating such legends and superstitions should be avoided in preaching and instruction (Miquel and Seyssel, *DS*). One does not find in Jane Owen's writing the influence of Catherine of Genoa, Teresa of Avila, John of the Cross, and other mystics (banned in England) whose works were inundating the Continent in Jane's times, describing the concept of purgatory as a state of soul where one already has glimpsed God and where the resulting Love and Joy become progressively more intense as the soul willingly becomes more purified, desiring and longing for fulfillment of Divine Love in the Beatific Vision (Miquel and Seyssel, *DS*). The concept is described in modern terms as the soul's self-transcendence and 'divinizing journey toward God' (Morrissey, *NDCS*). Jane, however, first tells her readers that she plans to motivate them by 'fear' of purgatory while describing it as 'dreadfull torments', 'an Eternity of punishments' (Dedicatory Epistle, n.p.n.), and then throughout the work repeating her description of purgatory as a concrete place with 'insufferable flames' (65), 'far more atrocious and intollerable, then any paynes or torments of this life ... ' (76), an 'infinity of torments' (112), with 'direfull flames' (114), to be avoided by prayer and almsgiving.

Jane Owen translated only the one chapter on purgatory from Bellarmine's jeremiad, *De Gemitu Columbae sive de bono lachrymorum*, translated as *The Mourning of the Dove or The Value of Tears*. In this work, the Jesuit Cardinal seems to follow the (pre-Council of Trent) Ignatian Spiritual Exercises, aiming to lead one to sorrow for sin, repentance, reform of life and love of God and neighbour, with hope of heaven and tears forgotten (Egan, *NDCS*), with which thoughts his work ends. The 'Tears' referred to by Bellarmine are not only those of personal sorrow but also of compassion for others, including those in purgatory, and his emphasis is not on personal fear, as is Jane's, but on the mercy of God as 'Liberator', releasing those in purgatory through the prayers and good works of the living. Although Bellarmine at first presents purgatory according to cited medieval legends of torture, he employs a method used also by many of his contemporary Jesuit preachers: taking their audiences 'where they are at the present moment' and leading them from their customary thoughts (in this case nourished by medieval legends), towards a self-forgetting love of God and neighbour (Miquel and Seyssel, *DS*). By translating and emphasizing only one part of Bellarmine's work, however, Jane continues a self-preoccupation found in popular trends of medieval theological thought, while Bellarmine's work reflects the theocentric emphases of Counter-Reformation theology (Bremond).

But Jane lived in harsh times of persecution, with torture or death as part of the civil 'judicial system'. She ends valiantly with encouraging observations that great good and great charity may result from harsh circumstances, and sorrow can be transformed into joy.

References

Adams, M. Clare, O.S.C. (1993), 'Tears (Gift of)', in *New Dictionary of Catholic Spirituality (NDCS)*, Michael Downey (ed.), Collegeville, MN: The Liturgical Press

Bellarmino, Roberto Francesco Romolo (Saint) (1721; rpt. 1870–1874), *Opera Omnia, Ex editione Veneta, pluribus tum additis tum correctis*, Tome 8, J. Fèvre (ed.), Paris: Vivès

Bremond, Henri (1916; rpt. 1967), *Histoire Littéraire du Sentiment Religieux en France, depuis la fin des guerres de religion jusqu'à nos jours*, I, Paris: Bloud et Gay

Cooper, Thompson (1917; rpt. 1973), 'George Chamberlain or Chamberlayne', in *Dictionary of National Biography*, IV, Oxford: Oxford University Press

Egan, Harvey D., S. J. (1993), 'Ignatian Spirituality', in *New Dictionary of Catholic Spirituality*, Michael Downey (ed.), Collegeville, MN: The Liturgical Press

Gillow, Joseph (1885–1902), *A Literary and Biographical History or Bibliographical Dictionary of the English Catholics*, I, V (rpt.), New York: Burt Franklin

Guilday, Peter Keenan (1914), *The English Catholic Refugees on the Continent, 1558–1795*, London: Longmans Green & Co.

Hamilton, Adam, O.S.B. (ed.) (1904–1906), *The Chronicle of the English Augustinian Canonesses Regular of the Lateran at St Monica's in Louvain ...*, I, II, Edinburgh & London: Sands & Co.

Lee, Sidney (1917, rpt. 1973), 'George Owen', in *Dictionary of National Biography*, XIV, Oxford: Oxford University Press

Miquel, Pierre and Chantal de Seyssel (1986), 'Purgatoire', in *Dictionnaire de Spiritualité Ascétique et Mystique*, Tome 12, Deuxième Partie, A. Rayez, A. Derville, A. Solignac, *et al.* (eds), Paris: Beauchesne

Morrissey, Michael P. (1993), 'Afterlife', in *New Dictionary of Catholic Spirituality*, Michael Downey (ed.), Collegeville, MN: The Liturgical Press

DOROTHY L. LATZ

An Antidote Against Purgatory is reproduced in the original size from the copy at the Bodleian Library.

AN
ANTIDOTE
AGAINST
PVRGATORY.
OR

Discourse, wherein is shewed that *Good-Workes*, and *Almes-deeds*, performed in the Name of Christ, are a chiefe meanes for the preuenting, or mitigating the Torments of Purgatory.

Written by that Vertuous, and Right worthy Gentle-woman (the Honour of her Sexe for Learning in England) M.s *IANE OWEN, late of* God-stow *in Oxfordshire, deceased, and now published after her death.*

As VVater doth extinguish fire, so Almes-deeds do extinguish sinne. Ecclel. 3.

Printed M. DC. XXXIIII.

TO THE WORTHY AND CONSTANT CATHOLICKES OF ENGLAND:

And more particularly, to such, who be of the best temporall Meanes.

WORTHY and Noble Catholiks: My charity towards the aduancing of the spiritual good of your soules,

THE EPISTLE

is the mayne Allectiue, inuiting me to write this small Treatise, (pardon I pray the boldnes of my Sexe heerin.) The subiect therof is, First, to inculcate, & make deep impressiōs in your minds, of the horrour, and most dreadfull torments of Purgatory: Secōdarily, to set before your eyes, the best meanes to preuent, at least to asswage, and mitigate them: gratū opus agricolis; A labour (I hope) pleasing to such, who are desirous to cultiuate their owne Soules, for gayning their spirituall and expected harnest.

That you belieue there is a Purgatory, your owne Catholicke Faith teacheth you; therefore

DEDICATORY.

fore presuming that you rest immoueable therein, without the least fluctuation of iudgment, I hould it were but lost labour, to spend any tyme in prooffe thereof. Only I heere couet, that you would deeply consider and meditate thereof; and thereupon that you would withall meditate and put in practise the meanes of auoiding the same.

Touching the terriblenes of the Torments of Purgatory, I haue insisted in the Authority of the most Blessed Cardinall Bellarmine; out of one of whose spirituall bookes I haue translated a whole passage concerning this subiect, as hereafter I shall

more

THE EPISTLE

more fully shew. Thus I make him the foundation or ground-worke of this my ensuing Discourse; and the rest following I do build, and erect vpon this foundation: so as this Miscelene worke of myne, may perhaps resemble the statua of Nabuchodonozor, of which, part was gould, part siluer, and part of baser mettall. So I am sure, that what is taken out of the learned Cardinalls writings in this my Treatise, is perfect gould or siluer; what is adioyned thereto by me, must (I willingly yield) endure the touch of the learned, to proue what mettall it is.

But now, to proceede a little

DEDICATORY.

further: I could wish you (worthy Catholickes) that you would haue a feeling apprehension of the paynes of Purgatory, *though yet to come. True it is, that the* Time present, *and the* Time future *are in nature different; yet if a man could in some case, so liuely paint to himselfe the face of the* Time future, *as that it might appeare to him, to be the* Time present, *it were,* felix Error, *a happy mistaking or confusion of tymes, (to vse the Catholike Churches like* Dialect *of the sinne of* Adam, *calling it,* felix Culpa:) *For then would men apprehende the Future paynes of*

THE EPISTLE

Purgatory, as *present*, (and certainely once they must be present;) and consequently, would haue a greater feare and dread of them, then cōmonly they now haue. It is not in mans power to depriue God of his incommunicable *Attribute* of Iustice, being euen of the Eßence of God.

This then being so, why will you not seeke to appease this his Iustice *in this world*, when *small satisfactions will serue*, rather then to performe *those satisfactions incomparably far greater in a more horrible manner*, in the next World, by enduring those Torments, which are not to be endured? And there to

endure

DEDICATORY.

endure them, donec reddas nouissimum Quadrantem, Matth. 5. *These are the words of holy Scripture, and are vnderstood in the iudgment of the Ancient Fathers, of a Soule lying in* Purgatory *, and therefore must be performed: which forcing words, since they ought to be most dreadfull to ech Catholicke, not performing his satisfaction in this life, I haue therefore thought not amisse (though I grant in a most vnusuall manner) to set downe in the lower part of euery page; that wheresoeuer the Reader shall open these few leaues, his eye shall instantly meete with the*

* 5 *said*

said moouing words, thereby to cause him to haue a more intense and serious meditation of them.

It is certaine, that God is pittifully cruell (as I may say) since he is content to turne Eternity of punishments, into temporall paines; But withall it is no lesse certaine, that a soule not performing its penance in this life before its dissolution from the body, can no more immedtatly ascend to Heauen, then the Patriarchs which dyed in Egypt, *could be buryed in the land of* Promise.

Well now, the chiefest help for the preuenting of the paines of Purgatory, *is the practise of*

Workes

DEDICATORY.

Workes of Almes-deeds, *and such other actions of Mercy, as hereafter in this short Treatise wil more fully be proued.* Workes *of this nature are the only Oyle, which is to be powred into a Repenting soule, whose full satisfaction for its former sinnes, is not yet accomplished.*

Gods *sacred Word assureth you, that you may buy Heauen with* Good Workes *:* Venite possidete paratum vobis regnum; Esuriui enim, & dedistis manducare &c. Matth. 25. *Much more then, may you with* Good Workes *(dyed in the bloud of our Sauiour, and not otherwise) buy out the paynes of* Purgatory.

* 6

The Epistle

sy. And though you do find a reluctation in your naturall dispositions to relinquish a part of your state to that end, now in your lyfe time; yet let that be made easy to you by Grace, which is hard and difficult by Nature; that so it may be said of you, as was said of Cornelius the Centurion, Act. 10. Eleemosinæ vestræ commemoratæ sunt in conspectu Dei. For assure your selues, that the Grace of God euer seeketh a charitable Hart.

And by this meanes, you may become more rich in your graces, then you could haue beene in your life tyme: Since to giue a-

way

DEDICATORY.

way riches, in a mans lyfe, for the good of the soule, is to carry them away after his death. And in this sense, they hould most, who haue the most open hand in dispensing of their riches; So true is that sentence, to wit, It is no small riches, for Gods sake, to abandon riches.

But (alas) such are the pitifull tymes, wherein we liue, & such is the scarsity of Vertue among vs, as that insteed of practising Workes of Charity, men are commended and praysed, if only they forbeare to practise workes of Iniustice and Wrong. And thus we are glad to accept of a meere Priuation of Vice,

The Epistle

in place of a Positiue, *and* reall Vertue. *O the miserablenes of our dayes! The very Beasts do not, nor can sinne, nor can they do any wrong; are they therefore vertuous?*

*Well, I humbly besecch you to haue a setled eye vpon your soules good, for the preuenting of future punishments; and remember, that our Sauiour in the Ghospell (*Luc. 17.*) commended the* vniust Steward *for hoording vp for the tyme to come; and shall then the slouthfull carelessnes of Catholikes be vpbrayded with that* vniust stewards *diligence? God forbid! But before I do remit you to the*

perusall

DEDICATORY.

perusall of this ensuing Discourse, I will put you in mind, that all Good Workes *streame from* Charity, *& that without it, there are no* Good Workes.

Now, how necessary and efficacious Charity *is in its owne Nature, it being the Queene of all vertues (the which who hath it, cannot be damned; and who wanteth, cannot be saued) I will not only refer you to the* Apostles *iust prayses giuen thereof (* 1. Cor. 8. *) but also to the learned and graue Iudgment of* Cardinall Bellarmine *herein, who thus writeth (* lib. 5. de æterna Felicitate cap. 6. *)* Audeo dicere, si oleum charita-

The Epistle

tis in animas damnatorum &c. I dare be bould to say, that if the oyle of Charity could distill downe into the Soules of damned men, or into the Diuells, we instantly should behould, both the damned Soules and the Diuells, to ascend out of their torments. As on the contrary side, if this oyle of Charity should forsake the holy Angels, Apostles, Martyrs, Virgins, &c. they instantly would become lumpish and heauy, & thereupon would descend into the lowest parts.

Thus you see, what this learned Cardinall *censureth here:*

DEDICATORY.

of. Do not then sleight and neglect the worth of this Noble Vertue of Charity; and particularly the most healthfull and fruitfull effects, proceeding from thence; I meane Good Workes, Mercy, and pious Liberality imployed vpon others; ascertayning your selues, that the next and most speedy helpe to procure God, to be mercifull, in mildly chastizing the relickes of your sinnes, & to mitigate your temporall punishments, is to shew your selues mercifull to others; Beati misericordes, quoniam ipsi misericordiam consequentur, Matth. 5. I meane prompt and ready in exercising

the

The Epistle

the Workes of Charity; since siluer in a large degree bestowed in this manner, is the spirituall Water, which quencheth the flames of Purgatory.

One thing heere I wish you to remember, that euery man (how yong soeuer) through the wingy speedines of time, is euen flying towards his graue. And when he is once thither come, then hath he bidden his last Adieu, or Good Night to all the world. Therefore whiles the day lasteth, employ your selues busily in Good Workes: So true (and withall wholesome) is that Counsell in Holy Writ. Eccl. 9. Quodcumque facere potest
manus

DEDICATORY.

manus tua, instanter operare &c. Whatsoeuer thy hand can do, do it instantly; because neither any worke, nor reason, nor knowledge, nor wisdome, is beneath whither thou hastest.

And with this (Worthy & deare Catholickes) *I remit you to the perusing of this litle Treatise ; Humbly beseeching his Mercy, that the reading of it may beget great and worthy effects in you ; And then I shall hope, that you will vouchsafe me now and then, your charitable prayers ; not only for the remitting of the guilt of eternall damnation, due for my infinite sin-*

nes ;

The Epistle

nes; but also, if so his Diuine Maiesty would vouchsafe me, (though most vnworthy) so much fauour and grace, that I may escape this most dreadfull fyer of Purgatory.

Your Soules well-wishing Admonisher,

IANE OVVEN.

The

The Contents of the seuerall Sections ensuing.

SECT. I.

OF the inexplicable paynes of Purgatory, and of other Circumstances accompanying the same paynes; translated out of the spirituall Booke of Cardinall Bellarmine, intituled; De gemitu Columbæ lib. 2. cap. 9.

SECT. II.

Of the meanes to auoyde, at least to mitigate, the paynes of Purgatory.

SECT.

SECT. III.

A perſuaſory Diſcourſe, for the putting in practiſe the meanes (which are Good Workes *) for the auoyding the paynes of* Purgatory.

SECT. IV.

Certaine examples of Good Workes, *to be practiſed for the auoyding of* Purgatory, *propounded by the Authour of this Treatiſe.*

Non exibis inde, donec reddas nouissimum Quadrantem.

Matth. 5. v. 27.

Thou shalt not goe out from thence, till thou repay the laſt Farthing.

Date Eleemosynam, & ecce omnia vobis munda sunt.

Luc. 11. v. 41.

Giue Almes, and behould all thinges are cleane vnto you.

Of the inexplicable paynes of Purgatory, and of other Circumstances accompanying the same; translated out of the spiritual Booke of Cardinall Bellarmine, entituled: De gemitu Columbæ. lib. 2. ca. 9.

THE I. SECTION.

AMONG all the Passions of the mind, there is not any, which hath so great a soueraignty, and command ouer man, as the Passion of *Feare*. The reason hereof is euident, and euen ingraffed in mans Nature. For euery man taketh pleasure and delight in a sweet and quiet repose of his owne beeing; and consequently flyeth, and auoydeth whatsoeuer may endanger to hinder, or take away his said quietnesse and rest; according to that Axiome in Philosophy: *Omnis res cupit conseruare suum Esse*. And hereupon it ryseth, that the *Passion* of *Loue* is nothing so potent and preuayling with men, as *Feare*. For we expe-

Reddes nouissimus ri-

against Purgatory.

rimentally see, that most men are afrayd to commit diuers impieties, more for *Feare* of punishment to be inflicted by the Law, then for *Loue* of God, or Vertue.

Now, to apply this to my present purpose. Whereas my proiect in these ensuing leaues is, to awaken the harts and minds of diuers Catholiks for the preuenting, or at least lessening the paynes of *Purgatory* by their *good deeds* and workes of Charity, performed in their lyfe tyme; therefore I haue in the Front of this Treatise thought good to plant a Discourse tou-

quadrantem.

An Antidote

ching the incomprehensible torments of *Purgatory*, and other circumstances accompaning the same torments; that so, such persons, for whose sake this labour is vndertaken, (as not being blindfoulded vnder the veile of carelesse negligence) may haue a greater *Feare* & Horrour of the said torments; and consequently, may be more watchfull and sollicitous for their preuenting of them, by their Almes-deeds, and other such workes of Charity.

Which kind of *Feare* was (as I may tearme it) the *Ge-*

Reddes nouissimum   nius

against Purgatory.

nius of Reuerend *Antiquity*, causing the liuers in those ancient times, to be so dreadfull not only of the torments of Hell, but euen of *Purgatory*: So healthfull to mans Soule is that admonition of Holy Writ, 1. *Pet.* 1. *Walke you in feare, during the tyme of your earthly habitation.* And vpon this ground our Forfathers labored so much to spread themselues in the doing of good works; and this with most iust reason; since he *is truly rich, who is rich in good-workes: and the want of them is a spirituall beggary.* And therfore most deserued-

quadrantem.

An Antidote

ly is this *Feare* stiled by the Wiseman, *The beginning of Wisdome*, *Prou.* 11. as also by some others, *The Mother, & Daughter of Wisdome*; and so holy Iob had iust reason to say: *I feared all my works. Iob. 9.*

The Discourse prefixed touching the Paynes of *Purgatory*, I haue wholy taken, and Translated out of one of the spirituall Bookes of the most Worthy *Cardinall Bellarmine*, entituled: *De Gemitu Columbæ. lib. 2. chap. 9.* Therefore when the Reader peruseth it, let him remember, that it is *Bellarmyne* who speaketh, not I. In this pas-

Reddes nouissimum sage

sage the learned *Cardinall* relateth certaine dogmaticall Miracles, touching the doctrine of *Purgatory*. I haue thought it much more preuayling to deliuer the contents therof in the *Cardinalls* owne words, which are without any affectation of Oratory, or fyled Speach, then by any other meanes or Method of my owne, in altering the same. Since I presume, that the speaches of so worthy, so learned, so pious a man (being an Ornament of this present age) will sway more with all good Catholiks, by way of perswasion,

quadrantem.

An Antidote

then any words of myne can effect; And certaine it is, that *who speaketh perswadingly, speaketh Eloquently.*

And I hould it a greater Honour, to become a poore Translator of any part of his learned writings, doing therby the more good; then to be accounted a skilfull Composer of Bookes, doing therin the lesser good. And with this I refer the Reader to the passage of *Bellarmyne* by me Translated, wishing him not to be diffident of the truth of the Contents thereof; seeing he may see, that the *Cardinall* giueth

Reddes nouissimum tum

against Purgatory.

full credit and assent thereto; and also, in that he is an ouer *Materiall* and *Sensible Christian* (as I may tearme him) who measures matters of Fayth and Religion, by the false yard of naturall apprehension. And great incredulity and dulnes it is, to thinke of things touching the soule, only as he seeth them, abstracting them from the trutination of Gods Iustice heere-after to come; themselues thus through supine heedlesnes falling vpon that dangerous sentence of the Wiseman: *Ita securi viuunt, quasi Iustorum facta hal e-quadrantem.*

ant. Eccles. 8. They liue as securely, as if their workes were of the Iust. But what doth there immediatly follow? *Hoc vanissimum.* This is most vayne.

The discourse of Cardinall Bellarmine, touching the inexplicable paynes of Purgatory.

THose Soules, who remayne in *Purgatory*, do afford to vs yet liuing in the world, a great occcasion & matter of teares; in so much that a due consideration & meditation of *Purgatory* may

Reddes nouissimum iustly

iustly be termed a flowing well of teares.

Now touching the paynes of *Purgatory*, foure principall heades or branches are to be considered; from the which we may in part coniecture of the greatnes of those paines; and in regard of such their greatnes, all good men may be the more easily induced, to powre out their teares in commiseration of their Christian Brethren, who are in the meane tyme tormēted with those paines.

The first of these Heades is, that the paynes of *Purgatory are greater & more intense,*

quadrantem.

then any *paynes*, which men can suffer in this *lyfe*. The second, that the paynes of Purgatory to them that suffer them, *do for the most part endure longer, then any paynes of this life can endure*. The third, that the *soules which lye in Purgatory, cannot helpe, or bring any ease to themselues*. The fourth and last Head is, that *the soules which are in Purgatory, are of huge number, and almost infinite in number*. Now from all these different passages, it is cleare, that the soules in *Purgatory* are in a pittifull state, and therefore most worthy of all commiseration; & that

Reddes nouissimum thos

those men, who yet are liuing, are no lesse then half mad and distracted in iudgment, who during their life tyme, are carelesse and negligent in satisfying for their sinnes, and had rather descend (vpon their death) to those places of Torments, then to be depryued of any pleasure, while they liue in this world.

And now to begin with the first, which is, that the paynes of *Purgatory* are greater, and more violent then all paynes ioyned together, which in this lyfe we can vndergoe; this verity is con-

quadrantem. Math. 5. firmed

firmed by the authority of *S. Austin in Psal.* 37. who thus writeth hereof: *Domine, ne in indignatione tua arguas me &c.* O Lord do not chastice me in thy wrath and indignation; Let me not be in the number of those, to whom thou shalt say; *Ite in ignem æternum,* go into everlasting fyer; neither otherwise correct me in thy anger, but that I may be made such, as that my said correction shall not be needfull to be increased with that purging fyer, in respect of such men, *qui salui erunt, sic tamen quasi per ignem,* who shalbe saued, but as by fyer. And then a litle after *S. Austin* thus fur-

Reddes novissimum ther

against Purgatory.

ther inlargeth himselfe: *Et quia dicitur saluus erit, contemnitur ille ignis &c*. And because it is sayd in the place aboue, they shalbe saued, therefore that fyer is neglected and litle feared. True it is, they shalbe saued by fyer: *grauior tamen erit ille ignis* (saith he) *quàm quicquid potest homo pati in hac vita*: Notwithstanding that fyer shalbe more heauy and intollerable, then any paynes, which a man can suffer in this lyfe. And you well know, what great torments diuers wicked men haue here suffered, and are able to suffer; yea good and vertuous men haue suffered as much

quadrantem. Math. 5.

as the former. For what paynes
or torments hath any malefa-
ctour, theefe, adulterer, or any
other wicked or sacrilegious person suffered, which Martyrs
haue not suffered for their confession of Christ?

 Therefore these Torments,
which are in this world, are of
a far more lower degree: And
neuerthelesse, you see, how ready and prepared men stand to
performe any thing commanded
them, to preuent the suffering of
them; with how much more reason then haue men to doe that,
which God comandeth them, that
so they may not undergoe those
 by many degrees more horrible.)

Reddes nouissimum

against Purgatory.

ble) *torments?* Thus far *S. Austin*, whose iudgment herein many other Fathers follow.

Saint *Gregory* thus dilateth of the same point: *Domine, ne in furore tuo arguas me &c.* Lord, do not chastice me in thy fury, nor rebuke me in thy anger. I know well, that after the end of this lyfe some mens sinnes shalbe expiated & purged by the flames of Purgatory; others shall vndergoe the sentence of eternall damnation. Neuerthelesse, because I do firmly belieue, that transitory fyer to be more insufferable, then any tribulation in this world; therefore I thirst not only not to be

---

quadrantem. Math. 5. aban-

abandoned and remitted to eternall damnation; but also I greatly feare, to be chastized in this temporall punishment of Purgatory. Thus much S. Gregory. Of the same iudgment herein, are Venerable Bede, in 3. Psal Pœnit. S. Anselme, in cap. 3. Ep. 1 ad Cor. S. Bernard de obitu Humberti &c.

S. Thomas of Aquin l. 4. sent. d. 20. q. 1. art. 2. doth not only subscribe to the iudgment of the former Fathers in this point; but he also further maintayneth, that the least payne in *Purgatory* is greater & more insupportable, then the greatest torment in this

Reddes novissimum world;

world; And yet notwithstanding all this, we obserue daily, that men are not afrayd to cōtemne those most insufferable torments in *Purgatory*, who cannot endure far lesse paines in this world. But this is the blindnes of mans corruption, which is much to be deplored in this our vale of Teares.

To proceed further. *S. Thomas* proueth this his former sentence and iudgment from this following reason: It is (sayth he) an inexpugnable and vndeniable truth, that *pœna damni*, the payne of the losse, incurred by

---
quadrantem. Math.5.   sinne,

sinne, is far more grieuous, then *Pæna sensus*, then any payne of sense, or feeling. And it is further most euident and confessed, that all those, who are in *Purgatory*, during their stay there, do suffer *Pœnam damni*, the paine of losse; that is, the losse of the vision of God.

But to auoyde the force of this Reason, it may be perhaps replyed by some, that the perpetuall punishment of losse, to wit, to lose for all eternity the sight of God (as such suffer, who are in Hell) is truly indeed a punishment and the greatest of

Reddes nouissimum all

all punishments; but during the tyme of a soules staying in *Purgatory*, the want of the diuine vision and sight of God, is not properly to be accounted a punishment, or at least not a punishment or payne more fearefull then those punishments, which Martyrs haue suffered in this life; seeing that we, whiles we liue here vpon earth, do not see God, and yet we are not said truly to suffer *pœnam damni*, any payne of losse; because we shall see God in due tyme, if so we purge & free our harts from sin, as is our duty to doe.

An Antidote

Yea the ancient holy Fathers, Patriarchs, and Prophets, who remayning in *Limbo Patrum*, expecting the comming of the Sauiour of the world, did not as then see God; and yet they were not afflicted with any *pœna damni*, because they were to see God in a prefixed & designed tyme. For thus Abrahā ansvveres to the Rich glutton, *Luc.* 16. *Remember sonne, that thou in thy lyfe tyme receiuedst thy pleasures, and Lazarus paynes, now therefore he is comforted, and thou tormented.*

In which words, we do not fynd, that Abraham said;

Reddes monissimum La-

Lazarus was tormēted with *pæna damni*, with the punishment of losse; but that he was in solace & comfort, & cōsequently not in torment. And further, where *S Simeon Luc.* 2. sayth: *Nunc dimittis seruum tuum in pace &c.* Now (O Lord) *thou lettist thy seruant depart in peace*, was not of opinion, that through death he should descend to any most insupportable paynes, but to a most sweet repose and peace.

To conclude *S. Gregory l. 3. moral. c.* 22. teacheth, that the ancient Patriarches and Fathers during their being in

quadrantem. Math. 5.

the place, called *Limbus Patrum*, did not suffer there any torments, but did find rest & quietnes. The force of this obiection or argument is easily dissolued. The answere is this. Whiles we are liuing here vpon earth, we do not easily apprehend, how heauy a matter it is, to want the vision and sight of God; both in regard, that what things we apprehend by meanes of corporall phantasmes, and the ministery of the senses, we do but obscurely vnderstand, as also, in that we being softened and cherished in corporall de-

Reddes nouissimum lights

lights and pleasures, we solace and content our selues therewith, and thereupon we are not much sollicitous and seeking after spirituall contentments.

The ancient Fathers and Prophets, were not tormented with any *pœna damni,* payne of losse, in that they saw not God; because they well did know, that this procrastination & deferring of enioying the vision of God, was not occasioned through any default in them, but because the prefixed tyme of that most blessed sight was not yet come.

But heere in our case, it falleth out otherwise, since touching those soules, who are condemned, and relegated (as it were) to *Purgatory* after the cōming of Christ, it is impossible, but that they should be in the highest degree afflicted; for seeing they in that state are depriued both of body, and of all corporall senses, they cannot take further delight in sensible obiects, as in meate, drinke, riches, honours, in satisfying any carnall concupiscēce &c. but they wholy breath and thirst after the contemplation of the first

Reddes nouiſſimum Truth,

Truth, and their enioying their *Summum bonum*, or *chiefe good*; for the obtayning whereof, as for their last end, they well know that they were created.

Heerunto may be adioyned this other reason; to wit, that the soules in *Purgatory* do wel know, that the kingdome of Heauen is now made open to the faithfull Christians, and that the only hindrance of not present enioying of it, is only the guilt of payne, contracted through their owne peculiar sinnes; from whence it cannot but follow, that these

quadrantem. soules

soules are euen offended & angry with themselues, in that they alone are the cause of their long dilation & deferring of their enioying so great an happines.

These soules may well be resembled to a man in great extremity of hūgar & thirst, though hauing a table before him furnished with all variety of meats, wynes & choyce waters; and yet the only reason and impediment of his not feeding of them proceedeth from some former miscariage of the said man, which hath deseruedly caused this his delay in tasting

Reddes nouissimum

of them.

We may add hereto, that the most ancient Fathers, *Austin*, *Gregory*, *Beda*, *Anselme*, and *Bernard*, do not speake *de pœna damni*, of the payne of losse, which payne all acknowledge to be most great; but *de pœna ignis*, of the paine of fyer; & this payne, they all with one consent affirme to be more horrid & intollerable, then any tormēts in this life. For althogh here vpon earth the torment by fyer is great, yet that fyer, which is not maintayned & nourished with wood or oyle, but is created as an in

quadrantem.

strument of Gods iustice, to burne and torment soules, must without all doubt be most violent, and sharpe in the highest degree,

Now, from the premisses it is euicted, that though we would not acknowledge *pœna damni*, the temporary payne of losse, which is in *Purgatory* (to wit of the losse of the vision of God for a long tyme) to be more insufferable then all the torments in this life; yet that the punishment of the fyer in *Purgatory* is greater then any temporall afflictions in this lyfe, is euidētly proued from

Reddes nouissimum the

against Purgatory.

the authorities of so many ancient Fathers aboue produced.

And becaufe, there are many men, who can hardly be induced to belieue any thing, which thefelues haue not feene, God fometimes therefore hath vouchfafed, to raife certaine perſos from death to lyfe; commanding them to relate to others liuing, what themfelues touching this payne haue feene.

Amonge fo many eye-witneſſes (as I may terme them) who haue feene the torments of *Purgatory*, I will alledge only two, the one be

quadrantem.

ing a *man*, the other a *woman*, whose testimonies therein are to be accepted without any doubt or diffidency.

The one then, is *Drithelmus* an English man; the history of which man *Venerable Bede* writeth, & relateth this accident, as a thing well knowne & euident to himselfe, it happening in *Bedes* owne life tyme, with great amazement to all of those dayes.

Thus then *Bede* writeth hereof in his fifth booke of the History of the nation of England *cap.* 13. *His temporibus miraculum memorabile, &*

antiquorum simile in Britannia factum est &c. In these tymes a most memorable miracle (and like to the ancient miracles) did fall out in Britanny. For to incite the liuing, touching care to be had concerning the death of the soule, a certaine Man being for the tyme dead, was after restored to lyfe of Body, relating many things worthy of remembrance, of some of which I haue thought good at this present to make particular mention. It is this.

There was a certaine Househoulder, or Father of a family in the Country-Norman, belonging to the Humbri. This man did lead with his whole house a very religious lyfe. Who being taken with a sudden infirmity and sicknes in body, and his payne more, and more increasing, he was brought to the howre of death, and dyed in the beginning of the Night. But at the appearance of the morning he returned to life againe, and setting himselfe vp in bed, all those, who accompanied that night the dead Body, through feare and amazement presently fled away.

But his wife, who loued him dearely (though fearing) remayned with him, whom he did comfort in these wordes.: Feare

Reddes nouissimum   not

against Purgatory.

not wife, for I am truly risen from death, with which this night I haue beene houlden; and I am permitted to liue againe among men heere vpon earth; but not after the same manner as I was accustomed heretofore to liue, but after a far different sort. Hereupon he presently did ryse out of his bed, and went to the Oratory, or Chappell belonging to that village, spending the most part of the day in prayer. He instantly deuided all his substance into three partes; of the which one part he gaue to his wyfe, another to his children, and the third he distributed to the poore.

---

quadrantem. B 6 And

An Antidote

And, he with great speed freeing himselfe from all care of the world, came to the Monastery called Mailros; and there taking the Tonsure, the Abbot prouided for him a secret cell, into which he entred; and there continued till the day of his death, in such great contrition of mind and body, that his very lyfe (though his tongue had beene silent) did speake, that he had scene during the short tyme he was afore dead, many things both fearefull, and to be desired. For he deliuered the matter in this manner.

Lucidus erat aspectu, & clarus indumento, qui me ducebat

Reddes nouissimum

&c. One of a lightsome countenance, and bright in apparell, did lead me. We came vnto a certaine valley of a great largenes & profundity, but of an infinite length. That part of the valley, which was vpon our left hand, was most terrible through scorching flames; The other part thereof was no lesse terrible through extremity of hayle, frost, snow, and wynds. Both these wyde passages of this valley were full of soules, of men and women, which seemed to be tossed to and fro (as it were) through force and violence of boysterous stormes. For when they could not any longer endure

quadrantem. Math.5.   the

the violence of so great an heat, the poore miserable soules did cast themselues into the middest of that insufferable cold, aboue related; and when as neither there they could fynd any rest, or ease, they then agayne leaped into those inextinguishable flames of fyer.

And whereas an infinite multitude of poore soules I saw thus to be tormented with this vnfortunate vicissitude of torments, and without any intermission or ease, I began to call to mynd, that perhaps this place was Hell, of the intollerable torments wherof I had before heard much spoken. My Conductour (who

Reddes novissimum

went before me) answered to my present thought, saying; Do not so thinke, for this place, which thou seest, is not that Hell which thou supposest. Now the vision of Hell, and after of Paradise, being explayned, which for breuity I omit;. the Conductour thus further said to the person raysed from death: Scis omnia, quæ vidisti? dost thou know all these things, which thou hast seene? The raised party said, No. I do not know them. To whom his Conductour thus replyed: That great vale, which thou hast seene most dreadfull for flames of heate and fyer, as also for insufferable cold, is

quadrantem. Math. 5.   that

that place, in which the soules of all those are to be purged and chastized, who in their lyfe tyme delayed from time to time to confesse their sinnes, and to make satisfaction for the wickednes by them perpetrated; and yet in the very last houre of their lyfe, obtayned true penitency and contrition for their sinnes, and so departed out of their bodies; which soules because they made confession of their sinnes, and had penitency of them (though at the last houre of their death) do yet belong to the Kingdome of Heauen. And many of these poore soules are much eased by the prayers of the liuing, by Al-

Reddes nouissimum *mes-*

against Purgatory.

mes-deeds of their friends, by their strict fastings, and especially by the celebration of holy masses in their behalfe; so as by these meanes diuers of them are freed from their torments before the day of Iudgment.

Venerable Bede thus further addeth hereto; *Cum ille incredibili austeritate Corpus suum vexaret &c.* When as this man rayfed to life, did afflict his body with incredible austerity, praying, and praysing God with hymns, he then standing in water frozen through cold with yce, his fellow Monkes would say to him; It is wonderfull, ô Brother Drithelmus, that thou

---
quadrantem. Math. 5.

art able to endure such asperity of cold; He then replyed, *Frigidiora vidi*, I haue seene much more cold places. And when they in lyke sort said to him, *mirum, quod tam austeram temere continentiam velis &c.* It is wonderfull, that thou wilt keep this austere cōtinency in meates &c. He answered: *Austeriora vidi*, I haue seene greater austerity. And in this sort, through an indefatigable desire of the ioyes of Heauen he tamed and subdued his old feeble body vntill the day of his death, he much profiting many by his perswasions and conuersation of lyfe. Thus far S. *Bede* in his rela-

Reddes nouissimum

against Purgatory. 43

tion of this history.

Now, that the contents hereof are most true, I little doubt, because it is agreable to the sacred Scripture, in the booke of Iob *cap.* 24 *Ad nimium calorem, transeunt ab aquis niuium: from waters of snow, they passe to ouermuch heate*. Againe *S. Bede* (a Venerable & most godly man) recordeth the same, as happening out in his owne dayes and lifetime. To conclude, there did follow out of this vision great spirituall benefit, the which God is accustomed to draw and extract out of such miraculous

quadrantem. Math. 5.   euents,

euents, and not curiosity or vanity, but the health of many soules by their conuersion to pennance & vertue. In this next place will I come to the testimony of a most admirable woman, her name was *Christina*, whose life is written by *Thomas Cantipratensis* of the order of *S. Dominicke*, a man most worthy of credit, and who liued in the dayes of the said *Christina*.

The same is in like sort witnessed by that Venerable man *Iacobus de Vitriaco* (*l. de vita & rebus gestis B. Maria de Ocgnies*) a pious and lear-

Reddes nouissimum   ned

against Purgatory 45

ned Cardinall, who in a booke of his maketh mention of diuers holy women, and particularly of this *Christina Mirabilis*, whose life he relateth most briefly in a short *Compendium*. Now this Virgin *Christina* doth thus speake of her selfe, instantly after she did rise from death to lyfe in the sight of many then liuing: *Statim vt è corpore excessi, &c.*

Presently after I did leaue my body, certaine Angels of God, being ministers of the light, receaued my soule, and brought it to an obscure, darke, and horrid place, being full and replenished

quadrantem Math.5. with

with the soules of men and women. The torments, which I did behould in that place, were so extreme, violent, and insufferable, as that they cannot be deliuered in any words. I did see there diuers, with whom I was acquainted, whiles they here liued vpon the earth. I did much pitty those poore miserable soules. I demaunded of my Conductours, what place this was, for I did imagine that it was Hell. They answered, that it was the place of Purgatory, reserued for such sinners, who had obtayned true penitency of their sinnes before their death, but had not yet performed any actuall satisfa-

Reades novissimum   *ction*

ction for their Crimes in their lyfe tyme committed.

After this, my Conductours brought me to behould the punishment of the damned in Hel, where also I did find certaine persons knowne to me in their lyfe tyme. After this I was conducted vp to Paradise, euen to the Throne of the diuine Maiesty, where I did behould our Lord wellcomming me. I reioyced excessiuely thereat, as being then perswaded, that I should there remayne with our Lord for all eternity. But he presently answered me, saying: Most welcome daughter, thou shalt without all doubt finally stay with me, but here I put to thee an election, of which of these two things thou hadst rather make choyce, to wit, whether thou haddest rather now stay with me for all eternity, or els to returne vnto the world and earth againe, and there resuming thy former body to suffer paynes, though without any danger to thy body, by which paynes thou mayest free & set at liberty those soules, which thou behoulding in Purgatory, didst commiserate & pitty, that so by this means, men and women yet liuing vpon the earth, through the example of thy penitent lyfe, abstayning from committing more facino-

Reddes nouissimum *rous.*

against Purgatory.

rous *Crymes*, and performing in satisfaction of them, what they ought to do, may in the end (being enriched with store of merits and good deeds) be conuerted to me.

Now I, without any pause or delay answered, that I had rather returne to my body vnder the former condition proposed to me; and thereupon our Lord taking it well, that I shewed my selfe so ready in the choyce, commandeth my soule to be restored to its body. In the performance wherof it was wonderfull to behould the incredible swiftnes, and celerity of the blessed spirits. For euen in that very houre,

houre, when it is sayd in the Sacrifice of the Masse, (which was then offered for me) Agnus Dei, O Lambe of God &c. my soule was placed before the diuine Maiesty, and at the third time of the saying of the foresaid words, Agnus Dei; the Angells restored me to my body. And thus the matter standeth touching my departure out of this world, and my after returne to lyfe; since all this was done concerning my being restored to lyfe, for the chastizing of men, and their amendment in manners and conuersation.

Therefore I would intreate all persons, that they would not

Reddes nouissimum

against Purgatory.

be troubled, or affrighted with such things, as they shall see in me. The things do exceed mans vnderstanding, which (God commanding) shalbe performed in me. Neither haue such euents at any tyme hapned among mortall men.

Thus much did she speake. And then the wryter of her lyfe adioyneth these words following, concerning her Cap. 6. *Tum vero cæpit illa exercere &c.* Then she did begin to exercise and put in practise such seucrities, for the performãce of which she was sent by our Lord: She did voluntarily enter into burning Ouens, & was tormented in those fyers; so as through the straytnes of the place and paynes, she made a fearefull & horrible noyse; But after she came out of those places, there was not to be seene in her body any print, or marke of such her burnings.

And then the foresaid Authour thus further proceedeth in his discourse *Cap. 7. Sub aquis* Mosæ *fluminis hyberno tempore, cum rigerent omnia gelu &c.* She very often & long stood in the waters of the riuer Mosa, in winter time, when it was congealed with frost, remayning there in such manner six dayes, and more.

Reddes nouissimum　　　　And

And then a little after the foresaid Authour thus further sayth, *cap. 9. Interdum in aquis orans &c.* She sometymes praying in the waters, was caryed by them vpon the wheele of a water mill, and so in most horrible manner was borne about with the wheele thereof, being notwithstanding perfect & vnhurt in all the parts of her body.

And the Authour thus more writeth, *ibid. Surgebat quandoque medijs noctibus, & totius Oppidi Trudonensis canes in se concitans &c.* She often tymes rysing about midnight, would stir vp against her all the dogs of the towne of S. Truyen, *she runing before them following her, like a swyft Deare, throgh certaine obscure places full of bryars and thornes, in so much, as she was pricked & her skinne torne in diuers places, as that no part of her body was free from wounds; and yet after her sheeding of much bloud thereby, no prints, scarrs, or marks of any wouds or pricks were to be seene in her body.* Thus far the forsaid Authour.

Now, that this his Narration of all set downe, was most true, appeareth seuerall wayes; First, because, as I said aboue, he had *Iacobus* Bishop and Cardinall of *Vi-*

Reddes nouissimum.　　　tria-

triacum, (a most graue man) to beare witnesse thereof. Secōdly, in that the authour of this History did relate passages done in his owne life tyme, and in the same Prouince, wherein himselfe liued, seeing he was Bishop, and suffragan to the Archbishop of *Cambray*. Thirdly, in that the matter and History it selfe euen publikely (as it were) deposeth and auerreth the truth hereof; to wit, that her body was so after conformed and strengthned by diuine power, as that it should suffer payne by fyer, and yet should not be dissol-

quadrantem.

ued; should receaue wounds and sheed much bloud, and yet no prints of those woūds should appeare.

In this sort this most blessed woman liued, not for the space of few dayes only, but during all the time of fourty two yeares, after her returne to lyfe. And lastly; because by this course of her life she conuerted many to true penance and compunction of their sinnes, and after her death was glorious and eminent for miracles: therefore *God* by such examples aboue insisted vpon, would stop the mouths of such incredulous

Reddes nouissimum per-

against Purgatory.

persons, who are not afraid sometymes to demand, *Who hath returned from Hell? who hath seene the torments either of Hell, or Purgatory?*

Behould heere, we haue two faythfull Witnesses, a *man* and a *woman*, who haue seene the most bitter and insufferable torments of *Hell*, and *Purgatory*; and therefore such men do wholy rest inexcusable, who do not bleeue these points: and yet those men are more inexcusable, who belieuing these & such like examples, do notwithstanding neglect, and contemne them, forbearing to

quadrantem. make

make satisfaction for their
sinnes to God, in fasting,
mourning, and bewayling
the most poore state of their
soules. But let vs come to o-
ther heads aboue specifyed.

The second Head was, *the
long and dayly sufferance of the
paynes of Purgatory*. I grant,
that there is a wryter (other-
wyse of a great name and
worth) who did maintayne,
that not any soule remayned
tormented in *Purgatory* a-
boue twenty yeares, yea perhaps not aboue ten yeares;
notwithstanding the vse of
the Catholike Church tea-
cheth the contrary, which

Reddes nouissimum pref.

against Purgatory.

prescribeth Anniuersary Sacrifices of the Holy masse to be offered vp for soules departed, not only for ten yeares, but euen for a hundred yeares, and more.

This point appeareth further from the vision, which we related aboue out of *Venerable Bede*, which sheweth that many Soules are to remayne to be tormented in *Purgatory*, euen till the day of Iudgment And the same verity may receaue its further warrant from the authority of *Tertullian*, a most ancient Authour, who speaking of *Purgatory* vnder the name of *quadrantem.* Hell,

Hell, thus writeth, *l. de Ani-ma. cap. 17. In carcerem te man-det Infernum &c.* Hell may send thee to that prison, from whence, vntill thy sinnes be expiated, thou shalt not depart, perhaps till the day of thy resurrection.

But *S. Cyprian Epist. 2. l. 4.* discourseth of this point more perspicuously & plainly, thus saying: *Aliud est pro peccatis longo tempore crucia-tum purgari igne &c.* It is one thing to be tormented with fyer for ones sinnes, during a long tyme; and other thing, to haue purged his sinnes through a mans owne sufferance and se-verity of lyfe. Which point

Reddes nouissimum

receaueth its further proofe from the vision of blessed *Ludgardis*, a most holy and eminent Virgin, whose lyfe was written by *Thomas Cantipratensis* aboue mentioned, who had written the lyfe of *Christina Mirabilis*. And because the matter is of Consequence, & concerneth much (by way of example) the Prelats of the Church, I will here set downe the words of the Authour himselfe, which are to be found in the second booke of the lyfe of holy *Ludgardis* (*apud Surium tom* 3. 16. *Iunij.*) The words are these.

Hoc ferè tempore Dominus Innocentius Papa tertius &c. About this tyme Innocentius the third, being Pope, after the Councell of Lateran was celebrated, departed this lyfe, and did presently after appeare visibly to Ludgardis. After she saw him compassed about on all sydes with a great fyre, she asked him, who he was. He answered, that he was Innocentius the Pope. But she replying with griefe said, What, is the Common Father of vs all, thus tormented for so long a tyme? He answered, I am in these flames for three causes. Which Crymes of myne had iustly deserued,

Reddes nouissimum that

against Purgatory.

that I had beene punished with eternity of torments; but that through the intercession of the most holy Mother of God, (to whom I did build & consecrate a Monastery) I had repentance of my said sinnes. And so it is, that I haue escaped eternall damnation; Neuerthelesse I shalbe tormented with most cruell paynes, euen till the day of Iudgment. That I am permitted to appeare to thee, thereby to intreate thee to procure prayers & suffrages to be said for me; this fauour the mother of mercy obtayned of her sonne in my behalfe. And at the speaking of these least words, he instantly

quadrantem. Math. 5. vani-

vanished away. Luagardis did make knowne this his necessity to her sisters, that he might be holpen with their prayers. But Ludgardis herselfe taking great commiseration of his poore state, did vndergoe wonderfull austerities for his reliefe. Let the Reader take notice, that Ludgardis did acquaint vs with those causes of this mans torments, which we for the reuerence of so great a Pope, haue thought good to conceale.

Thus much the former Authour, touching the vision of *Ludgardis*, which example hath often affected me with great feare and terrour.

Reddes nouissimum

against Purgatory.

rour. For if so laudable a Pope, who in the eies of men appeared not only good, but also holy, and worthy imitation, was in great danger of being eternally damned in Hell; yet in lieu therof is to be punished with most insufferable flames, euen vntill the day of iudgment; what Prelat may not feare? Who ought not to search most narrowly, into euery corner of his conscience? For I am persuaded that so great a Pope did not commit any mortall sinnes, except he committing them vnder the shew of some

---
quadrantem. Math.5. good,

good, was therein deceaued by his flatterers, & such his Domesticks, of whom it is sayd in the Ghospell, *Matth. 10. Inimici hominis domestici eius*: *A mans enemyes shalbe they of his owne household.* Therefore as being taught by this great example, let vs all labour to make most diligent inquiry into our consciences, for feare they be not erroneous, though to our selues they appeare right and sincere.

But let vs returne vnto that point, from which we haue digressed. It is not to be doubted, but that the paynes of Purgatory may be extended to ten, twenty, a hundred, yea to a thousand yeares. But let vs grant for the tyme, that those paynes should endure but ten, or twenty yeares; who is able to endure most dreadfull & inexplicable torments for the space of twenty yeares without any intermission or ease? Now, that those burnings are to be without any alleuiation or rest, appeareth from the vision, which we haue aboue'related, out of *Venerable Bede*.

Certainly, if a man were assured, that he should conti-

---
*quadrantem. Math.*5.

nue afflicted for the space of twenty yeares, without any intermission or relaxation, with the paine of the Goute, or of the stomacke, or the Head-ach, or tooth-ach, or of the Stone; & that he could not by reason of such his dolours, take any sleep or rest; no doubt such a man had rather make choyce to dye, then to perseuer, and liue in this miserable case. And if choyce were giuen him, whether he would remayne for twenty yeares without any respiration and ease in those foresaid paynes, or would suffer losse of all his

Reddes nonissmam state

state and goods; Certainly he would with a most ready mind, seeke to be depriued of all his temporall meanes, that so thereby, he might free himselfe from so continuall & cruell paynes: with how much more reason then, ought euery wise man to make choyce of vndergoing of Penance, accompanied with its fruits, which fruits are, watching, Prayer, Fasting, Almesdeeds, and especially teares, which are a signe of true Penance?

Now if we add to the acerbity of these paynes and the long continuance of them,

quadrantem. Math. 5. this

this third Calamity; to wit, *that the soules in Purgatory can in no sort help themselues,* their infelicity & misery is much increased therby. For here among men conuersing on earth, there is hardly to be found any one so depressed in misery and calamity, but that either by flight, or by resistance, or by mediation of friends, or by appealing to another Iudge, or by humbly beseeching the mercy of the Iudge, or by some other meanes, he may free himselfe in some measure from the vexations, with which he is enuironed.

Reddes nouissimum But

But (alas) in *Purgatory* the Soules can do nothing, but only patiently suffer their punishment. True it is, that Holy Men liuing heere on earth, may pray for the dead, may offer vp almes, and other satisfactory workes for the soules in *Purgatory*. But this priuiledge is not granted to the soules themselues being in *Purgatory*, except by a certaine Priuiledge to some few, and this most rarely; to wit, to appeare to liuing men, and to beseech ayde and help by their charity. Therefore the state and condition of those soules are

quadrantem. Math. 5.

most miserable, who being in those torments, cānot beget any ease or help to themselues, or to the soules of their Father, Sonne, Brother, Mother, sister or wyfe, or of any other friend lying in *Purgatory*.

But perhaps, It may be here suggested, that few are those Soules who come to *Purgatory*, and therefore the punishments there inflicted, are not much to be apprehended, but in a sort to be sleighted, and smally regarded. But to this I answere, *that the soules which lye cruciated & tormented in Pur-*

Reddes nouissimum   *gatory,*

gatory, are innumerable; and so many, as that the number of them is sufficient to moue and stir vp mercy, though their torments were far more easy and light. This is euident, seeing we are instructed a little before from the history of Venerable *Bede*, that *Drithelmus* did see an infinite number of soules in *Purgatory*, as also frō the lyfe of Blessed *Christina*, that the place of *Purgatory* was a most vast & huge place, replenished, & filled with soules.

Neither can it be otherwise, seeing nothing that is defiled, and contaminated,

can enter into the king-
dome of Heauen, but they
only, are able to penetrate
vnto the light of God,
(which is a light, and in
whom, there is not any dar
kenes) and to that place of
infinite purity who are truly holy and immaculate, &
are mēbers of that Church,
in which there is not either
macula, or *ruga*, spot, or
wrincle, *Ephes.* 5. Now, who
these men are, are most rare
and most few; and therfore
it followeth, that all others,
who belong to the number
of the Elect, are to passe
through the torments and

Reddes nouissimum paynes

paynes of *Purgatory*.

Now, from all the former passages of this discourse, it may necessarily be gathered, that the *Doue* hath iust cause daily to lament and mourne for so many mēbers of hers, which with an infinite desire thirst after their heauenly Country; and yet are in the meane time detayned from thence by intollerable flames of fyer, and are cruciated & afflicted with most bitter & inexplicable paines.

Thus far doth the Godly *Cardinall Bellarmyne* discourse of these former foure Heads, touching the Nature of Pur-

quadrantem.

gatory. Which discourse (in regard both of his Learning & Sanctity) ought to sway and preuayle much with all such good & pious English Catholikes, who are sollicitous, and carefull of their owne soules good. Now the Authour of this Treatise wil conclude this *first Section*, by adioyning a Reason drawne from *Schoole Diuinity*, which demonstrateth that the paynes of *Purgatory are far more atrocious and intollerable, then any paynes or torments of this life can be.* It is this.

 Three things do concurre as well to griefe or payne, as

against Purgatory.

to ioy. To wit; *Potentia, Obiectum, & Coniunctio vnius cum altero* (as *S. Tho. p. 2. q. 31. ar. 5.* faith:) An intelligent, or at least a sentient *Power*, or *Faculty*; a conuenient *Obiect* to that *Power*; and an *Vnion* or Coniunction of the *Obiect* with the *Power*. Now as concerning the *Power*, doubtlesly *Potentia rationalis*, a Rational *Power* or Faculty, is more capable of payne or griefe, then *Potentia animalis*, a sensible Faculty, or Function; For if we respect *Apprehension*, or knowing, the *Vnderstanding* in a *Rationall soule*, is (as it were) a mayne Fountaine;

quadrantem.

An Antidote

taine; the *Sense* but a small Riuer. So far as concerneth the *Appetite* or *Desire*, the wil of a *Rationall Soule* is a maine Fountayne also; The *Appetite*, (being inferiour to it) is but like a small Riuer. Seeing therfore the naked soule it selfe, is immediatly tormented, the griefe thereof ought to be the greatest, in respect of the Patient; for here in this lyfe not so much the soule, as the body is tormented; & by reason of the paynes of the body, some griefe and dolour passeth into the soule.

Now concerning the *Ob-*

Reddes nouissimum

iect; The fyer of *Purgatory* must be far more violent, horrible, & intense, then the fyer in this world is; seeing that fyer is created, and instituted, as an instrument of Gods Instice, who would shew his power in the creation of it.

Lastly, touching the *Coniunction of the Power with the Obiect*; the Coniunction of the Soule with the fyer in *Purgatory* shall be most strait and (as it were) intrinsecall. For heere in this world, where all things are corporall and bodily, there is no Coniunction made, but only by the touch of the Extremities, or vtmost parts of the bodyes, and the *Superficies* of things; wheras in *Purgatory*, the torments and fyer thereof, shall penetrate most inwardly the very soule it selfe. Thus farre, touching this first *Section*.

Of the meanes to auoyde, at least to mitigate, the paynes of Purgatory.

SECT. II.

Hauing in the precedent *Section*, shewed out of the iudgment of the most

Reddes nouissimum lear-

learned *Cardinall Bellarmyne*, the atrocity of the paynes of *Purgatory*, and some other Circumstances accōpaning the said paynes; in this next place it is conuenient to set downe the meanes, through force whereof the sayd paynes may receaue some alleuiation and mitigation: I imitating herein the Physitian, who first inquireth into the disease, & after prescribeth Medicines, for the curing of the same.

These meanes (according to the Doctrine of the Catholike Church) are these following: To wit, *the most* holy Sacrifice of the Masse, Prayer, & Almes-deeds, or good workes; according to those words of S. Austin (serm. 32. de verb. Apost.) Orationibus sanctæ Ecclesiæ, & sacrificio salutari, & Eleemosynis non est dubium mortuos adiuuari; It is not to be doubted, but that the Soules of the dead are helped by prayers of the holy Church, by the healthfull Sacrifice, and by Almes deeds.

With whom accordeth S. Chrysostome (Hom. 41. in 1. ad Cor.) saying; Iuuatur mortuus non lachrymis, sed precibus, supplicationibus, Eleemosynis. A dead man is helped, not with

---

Reddes nouissimum   teares,

teares, but with prayers, supplications, and Almes-deeds.

With which two former Fathers, Venerable *Bede* (to omit many other to auoyde prolixity) doth conspire in these words. (*l. 5. hist. c. 13.*) *Multos, preces viuentium, & Eleemosynæ &c.* The prayers of the liuing, Alms-deeds, Fasting, and principally the Celebration of the Masse do helpe many who are dead, that they may be freed from their torments, before the day of Iudgment.

But of these three seuerall kinds of *Suffrages* for reliefe of the soules in *Purgatory*, I will chiefly insist in shewing

quadrantem.

the force and efficacy of *good works*, or *Almes-deeds*. In the explication of which point I will first rest in the Authority of the *Sacred Scriptures*; Secondly in the iudgment of the *ancient Fathers*. And First, touching the sacred Scriptures, I will alledge diuers passages thereof, which although they proue immediatly the great vertue of *Good works*, and *Almes-deeds*, for the gayning of the Kingdome of God, and remitting of the punishment of eternall Damnation; yet (as the *Logitians* phrase is,) *à fortiori*, they much more proue,

Reddes noxissimu n that

against Purgatory.

that the Temporary punishments of *Purgatory*, may be taken away, and (as it were) bought out by the pryce of them.

Now, to begin with the testimonies of Gods Holy writ, we first read thus therin: *Eleemosyna ab omni peccato & à morte liberat, & non patitur animam ire in tenebras. Tob. 4. Almes-deeds free a man from sinne and death, and suffer not the soule to descend into darknes.* And in another place we read: *Sicut aqua extinguit ignem, ita Eleemosyna extinguit peccatum. Eccl. 3 As water doth extinguish the fyer, so do*

Almes-deeds extinguish sinne. Yea *Almes deeds*, and *Good workes* are so powerfull, as that our *Sauiour* after he had charged the Pharisyes with diuers great sinnes, yet thus concludeth, *Luc.* 11. *Verumtamen date Eleemosynas, & ecce omnia munda sunt vobis*; but notwithstanding, do you giue *Almes*, and behould all things are cleane vnto you.

And which is more, Gods holy word extēdeth the vertue of *Almes-deeds* euen to the Gentills and Heathens, for thus we fynd it said to *Nabuchodonosor*, who was a Pagan: *Heare my Counsell* (O

King) *and redeeme thy sinnes with Almes, and thy Iniquities with works of Mercy. Dan* 4.

Now, if *Good works* of Charity, and *Almes-deeds*, performed euen by Heathens and wicked liuers, be so much respected by God; much more then, *Good workes* of Christians and good liuers, are accepted of God, not only for the preuenting the paynes of eternall damnation, but also (which is lesse) of the temporall paynes of *Purgatory*.

To come to the ancient Fathers: *S. Cyprian* calleth *Eleemosyna, Solatium grande*

quadrantem. Math. 5: cre-

credentium, securitatis nostræ salutare præsidium: Almes-deeds a great solace of the faithfull, a healthfull safegard of our security. Againe the said Father, *serm. de Eleemos. Sicut lauacro aqua salutaris Gehennæ ignis extinguitur, ita Eleemosynis & precibus nostris delictorū flamma sopitur; As the fyer of Hell is extinguished through our washing in that healthfull water* (meaning at the tyme of our Baptisme) *so the flame of our sinnes, is abated by our good workes.*

To whose iudgment S. *Ambrose* alludeth in these words. *serm.* 31. *Eleemosyna Reddes nouissimum* quo-

quodammodo animarum aliud est lauacrum &c. Lauacrum semel datur, & semel veniam pollicetur; Eleemosynam autem quoties feceris, toties veniam promereris. Almes-deedes is a certayne kind of Baptisme &c. But *Baptisme* (meaning the Sacrament of *Baptisme*) is but once administred, and but once it promiseth forgiuenes of sinnes; But as often, as thou shalt do some act of Almes-deeds, so often dost thou procure forgiuenes of sinnes.

S. *Chrysostome* thus auerreth, *Hom. 25. in act. Apost. Non est peccatum, quod non possit purgare Eleemosyna.* There

quadrantem. Math. 5. is

is no sinne so great which *Almes-deeds* cannot purge, and take away. And more: *Omne peccatū infra illam stat: All sinne is vnder Almes-deeds*; meaning that *Almes-deeds*, and *Good Workes* can extinguish the greatest sinne.

To conclude, *S. Leo* thus writeth of this point, *serm. 5. de Collectis: Eleemosyna peccata delent, mortem perimunt, & pœnam perpetui ignis extingunt. Almes-deeds do blot out sin, destroy death, and extinguish the payne of perpetuall fyer.*

Thus we see, what wonderfull efficacy and vertue both the Holy *Scriptures*, and the *Ancient Fathers* ascribe & attribute to workes of Charity and *Almes-deeds*; from whence we may infallibly conclude; that since such *good-works* are of force to extinguish the eternity of Hell fyer, much more the temporary flames of *Purgatory*.

Heere now I hould it expedient to answere two Objections, which such men who are in slauery to their riches, not hauing the magnanimity and resolution to part with their siluer to any good and charitable vses, either for their owne soules good, or for the benefit of o-

quadrantem. Math. 5. thers

thers that are needfull, are accustomed to insist vpon. The first is, (say such men) *My goods are my owne, therefore I am not obliged to giue any part of them, but to what end my selfe best pleaseth.* Their second argument, and more potent is, *I haue wyfe and children, I am bound by the Law of God to prouide for them, and after my prouision for them, I shall haue nothing remayning to bestow vpon good and charitable vses.*

To the first of these two Obiections I answere; First, if we should dreame for the tyme that a mans temporall

Reddes nouissimum goods

goods were absolutely at his owne disposall, & that therfore it were in his power, whether he would giue any part thereof to good vses or no: to this I first say, that admitting for the present, that a man had sole dominion ouer his owne goods, and might dispose of them, as best pleaseth himselfe; yet certaine it is from the former authorities, both sacred and humane, that, that man who is so wholy drowned in his temporall state, as that he cannot endure to part with some reasonable share of them to pious vses, shall

---

quadrantem. Math. 5. hardly

hardly enioy Heauen (for without Charity a man cannot be saued) much lesse, shall he neuer escape the paines of *Purgatory*.

Secondly, I affirme, that it is a false ground to maintaine, that a man is so sole a *Proprietary* of the goods he possesseth, as that he may, as his owne passion and appetite carryeth him, dispose of them without giuing any part therof to needfull and charitable vses. And that this is most true, I produce in proofe thereof the Authorities and words of these Reuerend *Fathers* following.

To begin with S. *Bernard*, who thus speaketh to rich Men, in the person of the poore *(in Ep. ad Episc. Senonensem)* Nostrum, st pauperes clamant &c. The poore crye out, It is ours, which you wastfully spend; That is taken from vs most cruelly, which you (rich men) wast vaynly.

S. *Gregory* writeth in this sort (*in 3. parte Pastor. curæ admonit. 2..*) *Admonendi sunt &c.* Men are to be admonished, and instructed, that the earth, of which we all are, is common to all men; and that therefore it affoardeth nourishment to all men: in regard wherof they but

quadrantem. Math. 5.

in-

invayne and without cause repute themselues to be innocent therein, who peculiarly challenge to themselues, the common guifts and liberality of God.

S. *Austin* (*Tract. in Psal. 147.*) *Superflua diuiti, necessaria sunt pauperi; res alienæ possidentur, cum superflua possidentur.* Those goods, which are but superfluous to euery rich man, necessarily belong to the poore; Another mans substance is possessed, when superfluous riches are possessed.

S. *Chrysostome* (*Hom. 34. ad populum Antioch.*) *Non ad hoc accepisti &c.* Thou hast not receaued thy riches, to consume them in wastfull expences, but that thou shouldst bestow much of them in *Almes-deeds*. And againe in the same place: *Tuarum rerum &c.* O man, thou art but a dispenser or steward of thy owne substance; no other-wyse, then he, who dispenseth and distributeth the goods of the Church.

S *Ierome* (*vide Gratian. dist. 42. Can Hospitale:*) *Aliena rapere conuincitur, qui ultra sibi necessaria retinere probatur?* He is conuinced to take euen by violence, those riches which belong to others, who is iustly accused to retayne to himselfe more, then is necessary to his state.

S. Basill. (in orat. in illud, Destruam horrea mea:) At tu nonne spoliator es, qui quae dispensanda accepisti, propria reputas? Art not thou euen a Robber, who takest those things & that substance for thy owne, which thou hast receaued to distribute to others? The bread which thou hast in thy house, belongeth to the Hungry man, the Coate to the Naked man &c. *Quocirca tot pauperibus iniuriam facis, quot dare valeres:* Wherefore, thou dost iniure so many poore men, how many thou art able to relieue.

For greater breuity I will conclude with S. Ambrose,

Reddes nouissimum   serm.

against Purgatory.

serm. 81. *Sed ais, quid iniustum est, si cùm aliena non inuadam, propria diligenter seruem? O impudens dictum! Propria dicis? Quæ?* And then after: *Non minus est criminis, quàm habenti tollere, cùm possis & abundes, indigentibus denegare.* But thou wilt say? What iniustice is it in me, if so I do not inuade other mens substance, but reserue my owne proper riches only to my selfe? O impudent and shamelesse saying! Callest thou them thy proper riches? Which be they? It is no lesse a cryme, to deny to giue to the poore, when thou art able to giue, and dost abound; then to take riches from those,

quadrantem.

who already do enioy them. Thus far touching the *Fathers* Iudgment in this pointe, wherewith to shut vp the mouths of worldly and couetous men.

Now, for the better vnderstanding of the former Authorities, we are to cõceaue, that those who possesse riches, be indeed true Lords ouer them, if so they be iustly obtayned and gotten: if the Comparison be hœre made in respect of other men; yet with reference to God, they are not to be accounted Lords, or absolute *Proprietaryes*, but only *dispensers* of them,

Reddes nouissimum

them. For God created all things, and ordayned, that some men are rich, others poore; yet not in that sort, as some should be so rich, as that they shall abound with all superfluities; and others wāt necessaries, without hauing reliefe from those who are welthy. The reason hereof being, in that God being the Father of all men indifferently, did creat the world and all things therein, for the Common profit of all men; and therefore who retayne superfluous riches to themselues, without distributing part of them to good

quadrantem.

and pious vses, do contrary to the will of God therein, and consequently do sinne.

Now, to come to that other excuse, that *men are obliged to prouide for Children*, and *that therefore they haue nothing to spare for any good vses, thereby to redeeme themselues from the future fyer of Purgatory.* And in thus Apologizing for themselues, they can readily alledge that place of Scripture, 1. *Tim.* 5. *Si quis suorum, & maximè domesticorum curam non habet, fidem negauit, & est infideli deterior;* If any man hath not care of his owne, and especially of those of

Reddes nouissimum

his houshould, he denyeth his fayth, and is worse then an Infidell.

To this poore reason, shadowed vnder the veyle of naturall affection, and Paternall care, I thus answere. I do not disalow a moderate care to be taken for the prouision of Children; for he were an inhumane monster who should neglect the same. But this is it I say; to wit, for a man to be on the one syde so wholy absorpt & drunke in a thirsty pursuite of temporall riches, for a superfluous aduancement of his owne children; and on the

quadrantem.

other syde, to be wholy negligent, careles, & incurious, for the preuenting of the horrible flames of Purgatory.

This I say, is that, which may well be styled an insensible *Lethargy* in men. The *Extremities* I altogether dislike, the *Meane* I imbrace. And according to this (*O Catholikes*) your ouer great sollicitude in these matters, diuers of you will make superfluous prouision and charges in erecting a second House for a yonger Sonne, and the like; because they are neere to you, as being Prosemina-

Reddes nouissimum ced

ted from your owne loines;
But your owne poore soules
in the meane tyme you wholy forget, as if they were but
strangers to you, or (as the
Phrase is) but of the halfe
bloud: such cecity & blindnes in men is greatly to be
pittied.

Be not vnnaturall to your
selues, in being naturall to
your Children. Let your
owne Soules (which are
more neere to you, then any
Children) haue at least a
Childes Portion. When you
looke vpon your children,
looke vpon them, not with
an eye of an ouer-indulgent,

quadrantem.

but of a Christian Father: And then may ech of you say to your selues in an inward reflexe of your iudgment: *I loue you all dearely, with a Paternall loue, but I loue my owne soule, more dearely. I will prouide for your temporall meanes in fitting manner, and according to my degree. But shall my ouer much care of your temporall aduancement impouerish my soule? O, God forbid!*

What pleasure will it be to my poore soule, lying burning in the most dreadfull flames of Purgatory, for bestowing of that superfluity of meanes, which being otherwise bestowed for the

Reddes nouissimum   good

good of my soule, might haue redeemed me from those flames? Will your selues thinke intensly, of my such calamitous state, incurred by my ouer great loue towards you? and accordingly will you worke meanes, by prayers, suffrages, and Almes-deeds in my behalfe, for the lessening of those my torments? O, I feare you will not. And this I may probably gather, from the carelesse negligence in this point of many children towards other parents being now dead. And how can I promise to my selfe more from you, then we see by experience, other dead Parents haue receaued from their liuing children?

quadrantem.

dren? Let this be your speach in the secret Closet of your harts, concerning your children.

There is no Parent so kind, who would be content to suffer daily torments and rackings, to redeeme his sonne from the like torméts, to which by cómiting some flagitious Cryme he stands subiect & obnoxious. Is not then that Parent (I will not say halfe distracted, but) of most weake iudgment, who shall labour, and couet certainely to vndergoe most horrible torments (and incóparably far greater, then

Reddes nonissimum

this world can affoard) and this not for freeing his sonne from any paynes at all; but only that his children may liue in a more lautious, opulent, & full manner, then otherwise they should, though competent, and sufficient meanes would notwithstanding be left vnto them?

For is it not infinitly far better for the Parét, to leaue his children, in fitting degree and quality, furnished with temporall meanes, and withall himselfe, by distributing a good part of his state in his life tyme to spirituall ends, wholy to preuent,

---
quadrantem. Math. 5.

or at least partly to diminish the paynes of *Purgatory*; then to leaue his issue in greater affluency and abundance of worldly riches, and himselfe to continue many yeares in that insufferable conflagration of fyer; the grieuousnes whereof truly to conceaue passeth our conceite? O, *Ante faciem frigoris eius quis sustinebit? Psal.* 147.

Thus far I haue thought good to draw out, and enlarge this *Section*, in stirring the mould about the roote of this ordinary pretence, & excuse of Parents prouiding for their Children; by reason

---
Reddes nouissimum that

against Purgatory.

that most Parents (to the great preiudice of their owne Soules) do shaddowe their want of Christian Charity to others vnder this pretext; and therby they make their owne Children to become Enemyes to themselues: and so it falleth out to be most true, as is aboue alledged by the foresaid illustrious Cardinall: *Inimici hominis, Domestici eius. Matth.* 20.

Yet before I conclude this *Section*, I only say; although according to the iudgment of the Philosophers; *No man knowes, what kind of loue that is which Parents beare to their*

quadrantem. Math. 5.   chil-

children, but he that hath children; notwithstāding before I would endure an infinity of torments for their greater and more full aduancement, I would in part leſſen my temporall State, for the good of my owne Soule: for though Children be moſt neere to their Parents, yet that ſentence is moſt true; *Tu tibi Primus, & Vltimus.*

A Pet-

Reddes noviſſimum

A Perſuaſory Diſcourſe for the putting in practiſe the meanes (which are good Workes) for the auoyding of the paynes of Purgatory.

SECT. III.

IN the two former Paſſages are layed open, Firſt the Horrid atrocity of the paynes of Purgatory; Secondly, the meanes how to preuent, at leaſt to leſſen & mitigate them: It now followeth, that I ſpend ſome leaues in a *Paræneticall* (as I may terme it) or Perſuaſory

quadrantem. Math.5. diſ-

discourse, therby to inuite Catholikes to put in practise the said meanes, which are conducing for the preuenting of these temporary direfull flames. And whereas these my speaches are directed chiefly to such of you Catholikes, which are most slouthfull and sluggish in the prosecution of the same meanes, I moane, in the performance of *Good Workes*. Therefore I must heere intreate you, to pardon my rudenes of style, since it best sorteth to point forth (for words are the Images of things) your most deplora-

Reddes nouissimum ble

ble state herein. Dangerous wounds (you know) must haue deepe incisions; And matter of Tragedy (for I account yours to be such) is to be deliuered in mournefull *Accents*. Neuer ought we in this case to forbeare the touching of the member affected with a hard hand. O no. The Apostle indoctrinateth vs otherwise, in those his feruorous and fiery words, 2. *Tim* 4. *Prædica, Insta, oportunè, importunè, argue, obsecra, increpa &c.* To such Catholiks, which are feruorous in the performance of good and pious Actions, this my speach

---
quadrantem. Math. 5.

speach doth not extend.

But here now I hould it conuenient to marshall and range such men into seuerall kinds, to which men this my Admonition belongeth. The first kind of these are such, as are yet *Schismatikes* in the present course of their lyfe, and other Catholikes, who hertofore perhaps haue liued for many yeares in a *Schismaticall* state. Touching the first kind of actuall *Schismatikes*; admitting, that before their death, they become truly penitent of their former continuance in *Schisme*; for otherwise their soules are

Reddes nouissimum

against Purgatory.

are infallibly to descend to Hell, not to *Purgatory*.

But admitting (I say) the best; to wit, that they do dye in true repentance of their former sinne, which only must proceed from the boūdles Ocean of Gods mercy; Yet, what ineuitable Torments, and for how many yeares, do expect thē in Purgatory, if otherwise they seeke not to deliuer themselues thereof, in their owne lyfetyme by good workes? This point will best appeare by discouering in part the atrocity of *Schisme*, and a *Schismaticall* lyfe. For the

quadrantem. Math. 5.   better

better explayning whereof I will insist in the Authorities of the Holy Scripture, & the most ancient Fathers.

And to begin with Gods word, we thus read, *Galat.* 5. *The workes of the flesh are adultery, fornication, & Sects:* (meaning thereby *Schismes*) *They which shall do such things, shall not inherit the kingdome of God.* And in respect of the state of *Schisme*, the Church of God, is styled in sacred Writ: *One sheepfould* (*Ioan.* 10.) *One body* (*Rom.* 12.) *One Spouse*, (*Cant.* 6.) *and one Doue.* But now *Schisme*, as comming of the Greeke ver-

Reddes nouissimus be

against Purgatory 119

be χἴω, *scindo*, deuideth that which is one, into parts: Therefore as a member cut of from the whole body, ceaseth to be a part of the said body; so a *Scismatike* by open profession of an Erroneous Religion, impugned by the Church of Christ, ceaseth thereby to be a member of the Church of Christ.

To descend to the Fathers; Marke how they pen till out a *Schismatike*, or *Schisme*: I will vrge but two or three for breuity. *S. Austin* then thus writeth (*l. de fide & Symb. c. 20.*) *Schismatiks though they belieue the same*

quadrantem Math. 5.   *points,*

points, which we beleeue; yet through their dissention they do not keep fraternall charity; therefore we conclude, that a Schismatike belongeth not to the Catholike Church, because he loueth noe his neighbour. Thus S. Austin. Fulgentius thus teacheth, (l. de fide ad Petrum c. 38. & 39.) Firmissimè tene &c. Belieue for certayne, and doubt not, that not only Pagans, but also Iewes, Heretikes, & Schismatikes, who dye out of the Catholike Church, are to goe to euerlasting fyer. To conclude, S. Cyprian thus auerreth (l. 4 Epist. 9. ad Florent.) Qui cum Episcopo non sunt, in Ecclesia non sunt: who *agree not with the Bishop* (meaning the supreme Bishop & Pastour of the Church) *are not in Gods Church.*

Thus we see, what is the iudgment both of Holy Scripture and of the ancient Fathers, passed vpon the most dangerous state of *Schismatiks*. From whence we may infallibly conclude, that supposing the best, I meane, that *Schismatiks* do finally repent & dye in state of Grace, which is most doubtfull, considering their long inueterate *Schismaticall* liues; yet what imminent temporall tormēts (euen hanging ouer their heads) are ready to rush vpon them, instantly vpon the separation of the soule from the body, and to seize vpon their soules, for the satisfying of Gods Iustice? But seeing the state of *Schismatikes* is so desperate & dangerous, I am to be pardoned, if I sharpen my pen more peculiarly against the *Schismatikes* of our owne Countrey.

Heare then, you *Schismatikes of England*, who for sauing your temporall goods, will endanger the losse of all eternall good; How much do you dishonour (yea vili-

Reddes nouissimum

against Purgatory.

fy God) by perseuering in your *Schismaticall* state? Assure your selues (*You Schismatikes*) that it is not in your power to command at your pleasure, ouer Tyme & Repentance. God calleth euery one, but how often he will call, no man knoweth; and be you afrayd of that fearefull Sentence of his Diuine Maiesty: *My People would not heare my voyce, and Israell would none of me; So I gaue them vp to the hardnes of their hartes.* Psal 81. O most dreadfull Relegation!

But admit, God will giue you tyme to repent; yet the

strength of your Armies is to weake to bend that *Virgam ferream* of God's Iustice, by the which he punisheth with eternall damnation finall Irrepentance, and chastizeth sinne (if so all such points be not with good workes cleared afore in this world) with temporary (but most insupportable) paynes of *Purgatory*.

But yet to make you to cast a more feeling and intense Introuersion vpō your owne most deplorable states, Suppose a Natiue Subiect should through some temporall respect and end, beare

Reddes nouissimum him-

against Purgatory. 125

himselfe most traitorously towards his King, daily perpetrating some Act of disloyalty, and euer banding himselfe openly with other his professed Enemies; how could this Man in reason thinke, that his submission could euer be sufficient for his after reconciling to his Soueraigne, and obtayning Grace and fauour, & future aduancement to honour & Dignity? especially if the King were of that seuere disposition, as that he was euer accustomed to punish (though often in a lower degree then the offence de-

An Antidote

serued) ech act of Disloyalty and Disobedience committed against him?

And is not the state of a *Schismatike* far more desperate and dangerous? This man committeth spirituall Treason against *the Diuine Maiesty*, by his daily communicating in Prayers and rytes, with the Preaching Members of an erroneous Church, Gods designed Aduersaries: How then can he expect, with his so much gauled Conscience, to arriue to Heauen without extraordinary acts of Mercy to the poore, and other workes of

Reddes nouissimum

Piety in this world, or of suffering most exquisite and invtterable torments in *Purgatory*? Considering God is iust, and seuerely chastizeth euery sinne, committed against him; *Behould* (sayth he by his Prophet Isay) *I will be reuenged vpon my Enemyes, & will comfort my selfe in their destruction*, *Isa.* 1. And againe: *God shall rayne snares of fyer vpon sinners; Brimstone, with tempestuous winds, shalbe the portion of their Cuppe*. *Psal.* 11.

Poore wretch (I meane poore *Schismatike*) how wilt thou be able to suffer these insufferable paynes, and this for many yeares at the best, that is, if finally thou dye in true Repentance of thy former *Schismaticall* Course, who with such anxiety, toyle, & impatiēce art accustomed to endure the payne of the tooth-ach, or other torment in this world? And is the *Schismatike* so sensible of a litle payne in this life, & yet hopes he shall not be sensible of infinitly greater paynes in the life to come?

Therefore now in tyme rayse your selues out of this spirituall *Lethargy*, & awake; since the longer you continue in this your desperate state,

Reddes nouissimum

against Purgatory.

state, you do but all that time (admitting you finally dye repentantly) euen heap fuell together for the nourishing of your flames in *Purgatory*. Remember the *Wisemans* saying, *Eccles.* 10. *Languor prolixior grauat Medicum*. You cannot but know, that during your state in *Schisme*, you are wholy depriued of Gods Grace, by which we make clayme to Heauen; (*Gratia Dei, vita æterna. Rom.* 6.) since you wilfully depriue yours selues of the benefit of the Sacraments of Gods Church; which Sacraments our Sauiour hath in-

quadrantem. stitu-

stituted in his Church, as the ordinary meanes, or Conduits, for the deriuing of Gods grace into mans soule.

Well, I will close this point of *Schismatikes* with this one asseueration: To wit, that a poore *Motley foole* (be you not offended, for I speake the truth) to whome God hath afforded only the vse of his fiue Senses, is in far more happy state, then you *Schismatikes* are. This mã (though most despicable in the eye of the world) as through want of the vse of Reason, cannot merit; so he cannot demerit: You through your abuse of

Reddes nouissimum   Rea-

Reason, do not only, not merit; but in lieu thereof you increase the heape of your sinnes, through a daily coaceruation of your *Schismaticall* Transgressiõs. This man is infallibly freed from the paines of *Purgatory*, much more of Hell: You are assured to suffer the paines of *Purgatory* at least, God grant (through your finall irrepentance) not the paynes of Hell.

Briefly this man through the benefit of his Baptisme, hath his *Originall sinne* cancelled; & as for *Actuall sinne*, he standes not obnoxious thereto: You are indeed freed by your ablution in that sacred Font, from *originall sinne*; but then you repeale the worth & Dignity therof, by your actuall perpetrating of mortall sinne. I speake in the sight of God, *I had rather be one of these poore-rich fooles, so to call them, (for he is rich, who is assured of his inheritance of Heauen) then to be the greatest, and most wealthy Schismatike in England; being resolued to continue yeare after yeare, in this his most wicked course of Schisme; Quid prodcrit homini, si vniuersum mundum lucretur, animæ verò*

Réddes novissimum *suæ*

suæ detrimentum patiatur? what shall it profit a man, if he gayne the whole world, and loose his owne Soule? Matth. 16.

Well, in this next place to touch a litle vpon such, who are at this present actually Catholiks, yet haue perseuered many yeares in a *Schismaticall* state, before they were incorporated into the Catholike Church; what satisfaction and deeds of extraordinary Mercy to others are they bound to performe, to peeuent the paynes *of Purgatory,* or els to endure them for many yeares? This partly appeareth, from the vgly

quadrantem. Math. 5. state

state (so to call it) of a *Schismatike*, aboue in part descri-bed. And if he will not per-forme such abstersiue Acts of penance in his owne lyfe tyme, by contributing, shew-ing pitty, and relieuing of others; let him take heed, he fall not vpon that dreadfull sentence of the Apostle, *Iac.* 2. *Iudicium sine misericordia ei, qui non fecerit misericordiam. Iudgment without mercy is to fall to him, who will not practise mercy.*

Alas! Are you not men? Must you not once dye (and how soone God knoweth:) And are you not then to

Reddes nouissimum ren-

render a most strict accoũt for your fore-passed lyfe-time, euen to him, of whom it is said for his most exquisit and narrow search into our sinnes, *Scrutabor Ierusalem in lucernis. Sophon.* 1. *I will search the sinnes of Ierusalem with a Candle.* And will you then be so negligent, and careles, in preuenting that dreadfull time? Since God is no accepter of Persons, neither will Riches, Worldly pompe, nor any other such glorious miseries help a soule ready to depart out of its body, for the deliuering it *from Purgatory*, except great Al-

quadrantem. Math. 5.

mes-deeds (besides other penitentiall works) be performed in the life tyme.

Well then, my poore, and deare *Catholike*, who for many yeares, through thy wicked dissimulation in matters of Religion, hast most highly offended God; Imagine thy selfe, that at this very instāt, thou wert lying vpon thy death bed: (that bed, I say, which the *Prophet* calleth, *Lectum doloris*, (*Psal.* 40) *the bed of griefe*.) worne away with payne and sicknes, & not expecting to escape, but looking euery minute for thy last dissolution; How

---
Reddes nouissimum would

would thy Iudgment be altered? and wouldst thou not thus (in all likely-hood) reason and dispute with thy owne Soule? *True it is, I thanke God, of his most infinite and boundles Mercy, that as a straying sheep, I am at length brought into Christs sheep-fold, and I hope to dye (through the benefit of our Saviours passion, and of the holy Sacraments) his servant, and in state of Grace, and finally to enioy the intermi nable ioyes of Heauen. But alas, though the guilt of Eternall damnation (incurred by my long former Schismaticall lyfe, & by my many other infinite sinnes)*

as I hope, through Gods infinite
mercy, be remitted; yet temporall
punishment due for all my former said sinnes, in most inexplicable torments of Purgatory doth
expect me.

   My poore Soule must continue in those burning Flames
(how many yeares, his diuine
Maiesty only knoweth) for the
expiation of my said sinnes, before I can arriue to Heauen.
When I was in health, enioying
my temporall state in all fulnes,
how easily with a voluntary re-
linquishing of a reasonable part
thereof to pious and religious
vses, could I haue auoyded (at
least mitigated) these now in-

reddes nouissimum

minent and vnauoydable torments? Good god! where then were my Wits? The very plowman prouides for the tyme of Winter; yea the Ant (to the which we are sent by Gods word (*Prou. 6.*) to be instructed) hoords graynes of Corne for his after sustenance; And haue I so negligently carryed my selfe, as to lay vp before-hand no prouision, against this tempestuous and rugged future storme? O beast, that I was! Sweet Iesus, how far distant were my former course of lyfe and daily actions from euer thinking of this vnauoydable danger? I haue liued many yeares in fulnes of state: I

---
quadrantem. Math. 5.

haue beene labouring in laying out good summes of Siluer, to heap land to land for my Children to inherit. I haue liued (perhaps) in a most profuse or wastfull manner; I haue spent to much, to gayne the deceitfull fauour of the world, in sumptuous apparell, exceeding my state, in keeping an ouer wastfull house, and in ouer great & vnnecessary Attendance about me. By meanes of some, or all of these extrauagant Courses, I haue spent much; And yet not once did I euer thinke to bestow the twentith part of these superfluous charges to pious vses, for the preuenting of those flames,

Reddes nouissimum which

which within few dayes (perhaps few houres) my poore soule must suffer.

O wretch that I am, that haue thus senselesly so neglected this fearefull day! Here now my former pleasures, and Iollity are come to their last end and period. Gods Iustice must, and will be satisfyed; since nothing defyled and contaminated (except all the rust therof be afore fyled away) can enter into the Kingdome of Heauen. Whither then now, being encompassed on ech syde with such thornes of danger, & anxiety, shall I turne my selfe? To the world, and my former pleasures thereof? O God,

quadrantem: Math. 5.

the remembrance of them is most nauseous, and distastfull to me; since the fruition of them is a great cause of my future paynes. To my former greatnes and fulnes of my temporall state? O, that I had beene so happy, as to have made true benefit in tyme, of that *Mammon* of Iniquity, my wastfull spending whereof must giue fuell to that fyer! And we are taught, that, *Diuitiæ non proderunt in die vltimo.* Prou. 11. To my Friends, Kyndred, & former familiar acquaintance, which I shall leaue behind me in the World? Wo is me, they are as wholy negligent of their owne soules danger, concerning this

Reddes nouissimum point,

point, as my selfe haue beene. How then can I expect them to be solicitous & carefull of myne?

To thee then alone (most mercifull and heauenly Father) who art Pater misericordiarum, (2. Cor. 1.) and who dost crowne vs in misericordia & miserationibus (Psal. 102.) I do flye. Who tookest mercy of the Woman of Canaan, of Mary Magdalen, of the Publican, and of the thiefe hanging vpon the Crosse. Betweene the armes of thy ineffable Compassion I cast my selfe. Lessen, (ô Lessen) for thy owne honours sake, and the bitter passion of thy most Deare Sonne, my Sauiour Iesus Christ, these tem-

---

quadrantem. Math. 5.   porall

porall paynes, which now made for me. Let my present Compunction and Contrition of all my former sinnes (through thy mercy, & Sons pretious death) arriue to that ascent and height, as that my Sauiour may say to me with the good thiefe; to day thou shalt be with me in Paradise. So shall thy Mercy thereby ouer-ballance thy Iustice; For to speake in the Churches Dialect; Plus potes dimittere, quàm ego committere: and it is my Comfort, that I read in holy Writ; Suauis est Dominus vniuersis, & miserationes eius super omnia opera eius, (Psal. 144.) Our Lord is sweet to all, and his mer-

Reddes nouissimum cy

cy is aboue all his Workes.

O that I had beene so happy, as to haue followed the wholsome aduyce, giuen to me by way of Presage in a little Treatise, entituled, An Antidot against Purgatory: I then did read it, but with a certaine curiosity, as thinking it nothing to belong to me. But (alas) I now find it to be a true Sybill, or Prophet of my future Calamitous state.

Well then, seeing my owne hower-glasse is almost run out, let me turne my speach to you (Deare Catholiks) in my health my chiefest Familiars; & with whom I did most consociate in my former pleasures. There is no

difference betweene you and me,
but the tyme present, and the
tyme to come. You all must once
be forced to this bed of sorrow,
and be brought to your last
Sicknes. To you then, and to all
others, who are negligent in prouiding against this Day, I do direct this my charitable Admonition. You are yet in health, &
perhaps as improuident in laying
vp spirituall riches against this
fearefull day, as my selfe haue
beene. O change your Course,
whiles there is tyme. Let my present state preach to you, & suffer
these my last dying words to giue
lyfe to your future Actions; since
they preach feelingly whose Pul-

Reddes nouissimum   *pit*

pit is their death-Bed. Be not in the number of those sensles creatures, who are buryed so deep in earth, as that they haue no tast or feeling of things to come; *Nolunt intelligere, vt benè agant.* (*Psal. 35.*)

Do now therefore (Deare Friends) do now, what you can. Now while you haue tyme, heap vp togeather, that spirituall Wealth, which will buy out all ensuing paynes; and turne the Current of your former superfluous Charges, into the fayre streame of pious workes, that so it may affoard you water, for the quenchinge of those raging Flames. Consider how you shall be conuented before the seuere Iudge, frō whom nothing can be hiddē, of whō the Prophet saith: *Tu cognouisti omnia, nouissima & antiqua.* (*Psal.* 138.) He is not appeased with guifts, nor admitteth excuses, who out of his boundles mercy remitteth to vs (vpon our true repentance) the paynes of eternall damnation; but yet chastizeth vs with temporall punishment to satisfy his Iustice: *misericordia & veritas obuiauerunt sibi, iustitia & pax osculati sunt. Psal.* 81. Therefore now begin to spread your selues in workes of Piety. Lessen your temporall Pompe, descend in outward comportment vnder your

Reddes nouissimum selues

against Purgatory.

selues, and let your sparing charges by this meanes saued, serue to redeeme you from those horrid flames, which are hereafter to inuade you.

To these, and the like disconsolate and Tragicall lamentations in the inward reflexe of thy soule (*my deare Catholike*) shalt thou in thy last Sicknes be driuen, if thou seeke not to preuēt the danger in tyme. Therefore Remember, *that he is truly Wise, who laboreth to be such in his health, as he wisheth to be found in Gods sight, at the hower of his Death.*

But now to come to you

quadrantem.

other Catholiks, who thogh you euer liued within the bosome of the Catholike Church; yet the state of many of you is otherwise most deplorable, who though you dye in state of grace (though many hundred Catholikes, through their owne vicious liues and finall irrepentance do not) yet your Case (with reference to the torments of *Purgatory*) is lametable. Most of you are wholy heedles & negligent in seeking by your good Workes, and Almesdeeds to auoyde *Purgatory*. How many of you, whose meanes are great, might

Reddes nouissimum with-

against Purgatory.

without any stay after your Death, euen post to Heauen by your Religious dispensing of a good part thereof; whereas others, through want of temporall meanes so to be distributed, must stay long in *Purgatory?* O, that Man should be so treacherous to his owne Soule!

It is daily obserued (euen with griefe to all Zealous Catholikes) that many of you are ready to lay out great summes of siluer for the increasing of your temporall states; That others of you, who are deuoted to the contentments and pleasures of this World, to dissipate a great part of your liuing in fruitles charges: Some in gallantry of appareil, others at Dyce, in Running-Horses, in keeping wastfull Christmasses; your selues & your Cōpany feeding most lautiously vpon all variety of curious meates & wynes, whiles in the meane tyme your poore soules perhaps remayne, euen hunger-starued (as I may say) for want of spirituall nourishment. In all which courses it is be feared, that many, euen mortall sinnes, are by you committed, of the which,

Reddes nouissimum though

though you after haue purged your selues by the holy Sacrament of Confession, yet what reckonings are there remayning touching the temporall punishments attending such your sinnes? which either in this world must be taken away by great satisfaction performed by you, or els all such rust must be purged and burned away in the Horrible Flames of Purgatory.

Therefore it is not a simple Imprudency; It is not a weakenes of the vnderstanding; It is not a bare mistaking of the iudgment: But it is is meere Lunacy & Madnes in you, thus to aduance temporal respects either of gaine or pleasure, before the preuenting of those insufferable torments. And if any of you, who are of great states, do leaue a hundred pounds at your deaths to be prayed for, O, you thinke, you haue made a large and ample satisfaction for all your sinnes, and that after those Prayers are performed, you are sure instantly to goe to Heauen. A selfe flattering, and credulous conceit! Thinke of the custome of the Venerable Bishops of the anciēt Church,

Reddes nouissimum

who were vsed to tye a sinner to performe penance seauen yeares, for the committing but of one mortal sinne: How much different was their Iudgment, from your Iudgment herein?

Againe, what small a proportion hath this so niggard an Almes-deeds of yours, with that of the man restored to lyfe, and recorded by *Venerable Bede*, who gaue the third part of his goods to the poore, the rest to his wyfe and Children; of whome *Cardinall Bellarmyne* did aboue speake in the first section of this booke? Or how stands your Charity to good vſes with reference to *Zachæus*, ſpoken of in the Goſpell, *Luc.* 19. who after he had ſeene *Chriſt*, gaue inſtantly the halfe of his ſtate to the poore. Truly I ſpeake in all ſincerity; I knew two Gentlemen in Englād, who were but Eſquyers, (though of good ſtates) and yet at the tyme of their deaths (beſides many other moſt good and holy workes done by them in their life tyme) the one of thē did leaue to good vſes fifteene hūdred pounds, and the other a thouſand Markes. Therefore let ſuch

Reddes noviſſimum

Catholiks, who are carefull of their Soules-good, be vertuously emulous of such més deuotion and charity; and let them remember, that saying of *S. Chysostome* (*serm.* 37. *ad pop. Antioch.*) *Non dare, sed copiosè dare, Eleemosyna est.* But to proceed.

If any of you, vpon your iust Demerits, were to be racked for diuers moneths togeather; or if any of you were in the highest degree afflicted with some Corporall payne; what would you not giue (if it were in your power) to redeeme your selues from these torments?

quadrantem. Math. 5.

And yet the first of these paines might endure through the Clemency of the Prince, but few moneths (perhaps but few dayes) the other could not endure many yeares, through the extremity of the payne (for *nullum violentum est perpetuum*:) And will you then be so leaden, stupid, and dull in iudgment, as willingly, and affectedly to vndergoe (it being in your power, by abandoning in your lyfe tyme a little Drosse, to preuent them) such paynes for many yeares (perhaps for many hundred of yeares;) in reference and

against Purgatory.

comparison of which, all the greatest torments in this world (in the iudgment of the ancient Fathers) are to be reputed, as shaddowes, or *tipes* of paynes? where is mās vnderstanding, where is the light of his Reason? But it seemes, they are exiled, and in their roome, are imbraced a most sordid & earthly respect of temporall, & fading vanities.

Therefore I may well here demand; Are such persons Catholikes? Are they Christiās? yea are they men? who thus betrample withall carelessnes, and supine neglect

quadrantem. Math.5. the

the good of their owne soules, and rauell out their tyme in idle toyes and pleasures? Alas! what are riches, greatnes of state, a needles fruition of temporall pleasures, or that, which you call your reputation & honour (which with-draw many from doing of good deeds). able to performe?

Syr John Oldcastle being exprobated of his Cowardlynes, and thereby reputed inglorious, replyed; *If through my persuyte of Honour, I shall fortune to loose an Arme, or a Leg in the Wars, can Honour restore to me my lost Arme, or*

Reddes nouissimum   legge?

legge? In like manner I heere say to you, *Catholikes*: Can your Riches, your worldly pompe and pleasures, or antiquity of your House, and Family redeeme your Soules out of *Purgatory*? Or can this poore weake blast of wind or ayre, which you call your reputation (consisting in other mens words, passed vpon you) coole the heate of those burning flames? Nothing lesse, since these toyes (through your abuse of them) shall serue, as bellowes, the more to blow the Flames of *Purgatory*.

   I will vrge one reason,

---
quadrantem. Math.5.

which shall make you (*negligent Catholikes*) to blush, and withall to grow pale; for it shall force you to be ashamed of your incredible negligēce in this great busines heere treated of; and it shall put you (if so Gods grace be in you) in extreme feare of your future Calamity. I will take it from the examples of certaine most learned, pious, and ancient Fathers. The Fathers shalbe these following, S. *Austin*, S. *Ambrose*, S. *Gregory*, and S. *Bernard*; all whose pens were guyded by the Holy Ghost.

 S. *Ambrose* through the

Reddes nouissaum   ex

against Purgatory.

extremity of his feare of the flames of Purgatory, thus writeth (*Serm. 20. in Psal. 118.*) *I shalbe searched & examined as lead, in this fyer, till all the lead be melted away &c.* S. *Austin* through his fearefull and strong apprehension of this fyer, thus breaketh out in words (*in explic. Psal. 27.*) *O Lord, let me be made such, as that my Correction shall not be needfull to be increas'd with that purging fyer, in respect of such men, qui salui erunt. sic tamen quasi per ignem*. And againe S. *Austin* thus further saith (*l 50. homil. 16.*) *O how happy are they, that who liuing*

quadrantem. Math. 5. well,

well, and contented with necessary riches to their bodies, liberall of their owne, chast in themselues, and not cruell to others, do redeeme themselues from this fiery Fornace? Of which fyer the said S. Austin thus saith: *in Psal. 27. Grauior erit hic ignis, quàm quis potest pati in hac vita.* This fyer shalbe more intollerable, then any man can suffer in this lyfe.

S. Gregory thus writeth (*in Psal. 3. Pænit.*) I esteeme the purging fyer (though it be transitory) to be more intollerable, then all tribulations, which in this life may be suffered; therefore I do not only desire, not to

Reddes nouissimum be

be rebuked in the fury of eternal damnation; but also I greatly feare to be purged in the wrath of transitory Corrections.

Lastly, to come to *S. Bernard*, whose trembling penne through feare of the paynes of *Purgatory*, thus discourseth: (*Serm. de sex tribul.* 16. *& 55. in Cant.*) *O would to God, that some man would now before hand, prouide for my head abundance of water, and to myne eyes a fountayne of teares; that so perhaps the burning fyer should take no hold, where running teares had clensed before.*

And now to reflect a little vpon the Worth of these

quadrantem. Math. 5. foure

foure former alledged Fathers; and then to draw our inference and deduction. S. *Ambrose* for his learning (he writing many bookes in defence of the Christian Fayth) as also for his sanctimony of lyfe, obtayned the title of being called (*per Excellentiam*) *One of the foure Fathers of the Primitive Church.*

S. *Austin* (gayning the like title) was of that eminency for learning and piety, that *S. Ierome*, thus extolleth him: (*Tom. 2. Ep. 25. inter opera August.*) *I haue allwayes reuerenced thy Sanctity with that honour, which is fit-*

Reddes nouissimum ting,

ting; and I haue loued our Lord and Sauiour dwelling in thee.

Thus much briefly of *S. Austin*, whose infinite paines, labour, and study (besides his extraordinary holynes in his conuersation & course of lyfe) in writing of so many, and so great *Tomes*, with such wonderfull perfection of iudgment & learning, and all in defence of the Christian and Catholike Faith, might seeme in the eye of many, to be sufficient to expiate the temporall punishment due for his sinnes.

S. Gregory was our *Apostle*, first planting Christianity in

quadrantem. Math.5.

An Antidote

England, and of that Piety, as that *M. Godwin* the Protestant (*in his Catalogue of Bishops. pag. 3.*) thus commendeth him: *That blessed & holy Father S. Gregory.*

To come to *S. Bernard*: This blessed man (as *Osiander witnesseth in his Epitome p. 309.*) was an Abbot, authour of many monasteries, both in France & Flanders, instituting *a Religious Order* in Gods Church: Yea he was eminent for working of Miracles; of whom in regard of his piety of life, euen *D. Whitaker* our Aduersary (*lib. de Eccl. pag. 338.*) thus celebrateth his worth: *Ego quidem Bernardum verè fuisse sanctum existimo.*

Now, if these foure most worthy shining Lamps in the Church of God (or rather so many bright stars in the celestiall Spheare) remarkable for learning, and more remarkable for piety and deuotion; they spending their whole tyme in writing in defence of the true Religion; betrapling vnder their feet all temporall Honours and Preferments; liuing most chastly in Purity of body, & wearing themselues out in Fasting, Prayer, and seuerely

quadrantem. pu-

punishing their owne flesh: Yf these men I say) notwithstanding all this their rigorous course to flesh & bloud did stand in such feare and horrour of the torments of *Purgatory* (as we see aboue, by their owne words and writings, they did;) what then (*My deare Catholickes*) may be said of most of you, who enioy the pleasures of the world, pamper your bodies, liue in great riches and abundance, & yet do thinke to escape the flames of that fyer? what is this, but madnes and incredible partiality in the highest degree; you be-

Reddes nouissimum

ing thus become *Parasytes* to your owne selues, in thus flattering your owne most fearefull state?

But it may be, there are some of you, who, so you may enioy Heauen eternally in the end, become thereby lesse carefull of preuenting the temporall paynes of *Purgatory*, sleighting the consideration of them. But *S. Austin* shall discouer this vanity, who thus discourseth of this point, *serm. 41. de sanctis. Some vse to say, I care not greatly how long soeuer I stay in passing this fyer; seeing at the last, I shall attayne to life euerlasting.*

To which words S. Austin thus answereth: *But alas, (deare Brother) Let no man say thus, for that this Purgatory fyer is more sharpe, then any punishment, which in this lyfe can be seene, imagined, or felt. And wheras it is said of the day of Iudgment: That one day shalbe as a thousand yeares, and a thousand yeares as one day; how doth any man know, whether his passage through this fyer be for dayes, months, or perhaps yeares? And he, that will now be loath to put one of his fingers into burning fyer, ought to feare the torment of that fyer, though it were but for a litle tyme. Therefore*

Reddes nouissimum

against Purgatory.

let every man labour with all his force, that he may auoyde mortall sinnes, which cast men into Hell; and to redeeme lesser sinnes by good workes, so as no part of them remayne to be consumed by that fyer. And then a litle after in the same place: *Who commit litle, and daily sinnes, let them not ceasse daily to redeeme them with good works; to wit, by continuall Prayer, frequent Fastings, & large Almes.*

Thus this blessed Father seriously meditateth in the secret of his soule vpon this point. What may we say of such men, as read this, and are nothing moued therewith?

quadrantem.

with? Truly such men may be thought to haue but the outward shape, or faces of men; that is, they weare fayre Cloaths, they talke, they walke togeather, they busy their minds in needles toyes; but as for the true vse of *Reason* (wherein the essence of man consisteth) so far forth as it may become seruiceable to the aduancement and spirituall good of their soules, they participate in their actiõs more with beasts who want soules, then with *Rationall Creatures:* A griefe not to be expressed, but in most deplorable *Threnes* and

Reddes nouissimum. La

Lamentations.

Nay, I dare be bold to say, that *Beasts* seeme to haue greater practise of *Reason*, then diuers of these men haue. Strike a Horse, or an Asse once or twyce, or thrust him into a deep or dangerous hole, out of which he can hardly get; he will conceaue such *Feare* thereof, as that he will for a long tyme after seeke to auoyde both the stroakes, and the hole: And yet, where the Scripture, the testimonies of the Ancient and holy Fathers, the seuerall miracles exhibited in proofe of the torments of

Purgatory, do fully proclame the horriblenes of those paines, diuers *Catholikes* who are infallibly hereafter to endure the same paynes (if so they make no preuention in their lyfe tyme) haue no *Feare*, no *Sense*, no *Feeling thereof*. O God, that *Men* should thus cease to be *Men*, and *Beasts* (after a certaine manner) should step in their place.

Well, I will conclude this my discourse to you (*Worthy Catholikes*) humbly beseeching you, euen for the most precious, and bitter Passion of our Lord and Sauiour, & for the future good of your

Reddes nouissimum owne

owne soules, to cast your eye
vpon all the Premisses set
downe in this smal Treatise,
and haue a feeling Considera-
ration both of the extremities of the paynes, and of the
infallible authorities pro-
uing the vndoubted certay-
nety of those paynes; and do
not suffer your iudgments to
fluctuate or wauer, touching
the certainty of them. Therfore, I will only demand, Is
there a *Heauen?* Is there a
Hell? Is there a *Purgatory?* Yf
you belieue these things to
haue a true and reall being,
(as no doubt infallibly you
do) where then (through

quadrantem.

your so much sleighting of them) is your Iudgment? If you hould them (as God forbid) but as intentionall and aëry Speculations of the braine, where is your Fayth? And a most miserable Election it is, whether a man will be damned for all eternity, for want of practising necessary points of Christian Religion; or through want of Fayth.

But before I end this passage I will turne my penne, but withall gentle, and soften in part my style, in respect of the Persons to which I will direct these few ensu-

Reddes novissimum

ing lynes. To you then (*great Catholick Ladyes*) and other *Catholicke Gentle-women* of worth (to whom in regard of my Sexe, I may be the more bold to speake freely) whose present Widdowed states by reason of your deceased Husbands, stand enriched with more then ordinary affluency (during your liues.) of lands, money, and other temporall goods: You I say (*Noble Ladyes, and others of Worth*) though you be weake in Nature, yet know your owne strength, and what great matters during your Widowhoods you are

are able, through Gods assistance to performe, for the freeing you from the flames of *Purgatory:* and remember, that howsoeuer the nycenes & delicacy of diuers of you be such, as that in this world, you can brooke nothing displeasing to you; yet in the next world, admitting you dye in state of Saluation, you must infallibly vndergo those horrible flames (so much spoken of in these leaues) except by your charitablenes (and this in a most full degree) you redeeme those paynes.

 O what good Workes

Reddes nouissimum   might

might you do during your Widdowhoods? And yet I feare, you are most forgetfull therein. Many of you (I know) are ready to bestow a hundred Marks, or more, vpon one gowne; and that gowne must not serue two yeares, but another (as chargeable) must instantly be had. Agayne, some of you will be content to lose a hundred marks, or more, in one night at Gleeke; and will weare about your necks Iewels, worth many hundreds of pounds.

O cut of these needles & fruitles charges, and bestow

quadrantem. Math. 5.

a good part thereof vpon your Soules, with the preciousnes of good and satisfying works, though your bodies in part be depriued of such glorious Ornaments. There is none of you, but besides your greater sinnes, you daily commit lesser sinnes; for it is said in holy Writ, *Prou.* 24. *The iust man shall fall seauen tymes a day.* How many idle, and vnnecessary thoughts and words passe from you, but in one day? and yet you must make satisfaction for euery such thought or word, either here or in *Purgatory*, before you

Reddes nouissimum can

against Purgatory.

can arriue to Heauen. For it is sayd, *Prou.* 19. *They shall render an account of euery idle Word, in the day, of iudgment.*

Now then in tyme of your Widowhoods, lay out a great part of your riches to spirituall vsury (as I may terme it) for the good of your Soules. I did know a yong gentle-woman, now dead: she was left by her deceased Father two thousand pounds, and better in portion. She intended to mary (and so before her death she did.) yet before she would subiect her-selfe, and her state to any man, (besides diuers good

quadrantem. Math. 5.

acts before) she gaue at one tyme (I speake of certaine and particular knowledge) three hundred pounds of her portion away, to the bringing vp of poore schollers beyond the Seas; saying thus to herselfe; *If I shalbe content to enthrall my selfe, & seauenteene hundred pounds at least, to the will of a stranger, who I know not how he will vse me; haue I not reason to giue three hundred pounds away to my owne Soule, for his sake, who will not suffer a cup of could water giuen in his name, to be vnrewarded?*

This is an Example wor-

Reddes nouissimum thy

thy of your taking notice of, thereby to put you in mind, to remember to preuent the flames of *Purgatory*, during the tyme of your Widowhoods. For if you be not solicitous thereof before your second mariage, when your states are in your owne disposall; it is much to be feared, that your future Husbands will bridle you of all such (though most necessary) charges. This Example may also be worthily a President for all other yong Catholike gentle-women of great portions, to prouide for the good of their soules,

quadrantem. Math. 5. before

before they tye themselues in mariage to any one.

Well (*Worthy Ladyes*) let a Woman once preach to women, and since you are Women. Imitate that *Blessed Woman* so much celebrated for her charity to others, in Gods holy writ, *Prou.* 31. *Manum suam aperuit inopi, &c.* She opened her hands to those that wanted, and stretch'd out her armes to the poore; and thereupon it followeth of her in the said word of God *Et ridebit in die nouissimo*; and she shall laugh at the last day, That is, at the day of her death she shall reioyce: and so

---
Reddes nouissimum (Noble

(*Noble Ladyes, and others*) it is in your power (if your selues will) to enioye the like felicity and retaliation, for your workes of charity, with her. And with this I giue a full close to this my *Exhortatiue Discourse*.

Certaine examples of good works to be practised, for the auoyding of Purgatory, propounded by the Authour of this Treatise.

SECT. IV.

THE first of these *Good Workes*, so much wished

quadrantem. Math. 5.

by me, shalbe not only in a mans priuate Deuotions & Prayers; but also by soliciting of others of our Catholike Clergy (though euen of their owne most ready propension and loyalty herein, I know they are not wanting) to pray for his *Maiesty of England*, our most gratious *King*, and for his worthy *Queene*, and their Royall Issue.

This is the Duty, which all Subiects (of what Religion soeuer) ought to performe; and the performance thereof is a pleasing, & most gratefull spirituall Sacrifice

against Purgatory. 189

to the *Diuine Maiesty*, and a good meanes (among others) to expiate our former Transgressions; *Thus shall ech of vs feare the Lord, and honour the King. Prou.* 24. And, *giue to Cesar, what is Cæsars. Matth.* 22. For if the Prophet *Ieremy* (sterned by Gods holy spirit, and therefore spoake the truth) commanded the *Israelits*, being brought into Captiuity to *Babylon*, to pray for the good state thereof, saying to them; *In the peace therof, you shall haue peace. Ierem.* 29. And if further also the *Israelites* be counselled by God in his holy Writ, to

*quadrantem. Math.*5: pray

pray for the life of *Nabuchodonosor*, and his sonne *Baltasar*. *Baruch* 1. How much more Reason then, haue all Priests, and Catholikes in England, euen to besiege the eares of God with their daily and incessant Prayers and impetrations, for the spirituall and temporall good of their King *Charles*?

Since the *Israelites* then prayed for their Enemy; We pray for our Dread Soueraigne. They for him, who did lead them into Captiuity: We for him, who keepes vs in liberty, peace, & tranquillity. They for a meere

Reddes nouissimum stran-

stranger and Idolater; We being Christiãs, for our Natiue Christian Prince. Finally, they for a forrayne Nation: We for our owne Coũtry, in which we are bred & brought vp, and to which we owe *Omnes omnium charitates*: So willingly we must remember, that it is said, 1. *Pet.*3. *We ought to be subiect to the King, as excelling.*

Therefore in regard of so worthy a worke, which euen in duty ought to be performed by all English Catholikes and Priests; I the poore authour of this Treatise, will make bold, though a woman to Personate all the English Priests and good Catholikes in my selfe, and will offer vp to the Highest (in behalfe of vs all) this our most zealous and daily prayer: *God preserue with his eye of Vigilancy, and care our most Noble Prince King Charles, and his most illustrious Queene, and most worthy Issue. God grant him to prosper in all true felicity, both temporall and spirituall; and giue him the Priuiledg that he may in his Succes-sours perpetuate his Issue from generation to generation: That so of him it may be sayd with the Prophet, Psal. 127. Filij tui sicut nouellæ oliuarum, in circuitu*

Reddes nouissimum mensæ

mensæ tuæ. And grant, that in the close of their liues, they may all leaue the Stage or Theater of this world with spirituall Trophees and Triumphs, for the gayning of that Celestiall Kingdome; in compare of which, all the kingdomes vpon the Earth deserue not to be Types or adumbrations. And, to this my vnfeigned Prayer, i wish all good English Priests, and Catholikes to say, *Amen.*

Now I will I descend to other pious deeds, and such as consist in charges of siluer. And heere I will insist (by way of Example) in certaine courses taken by diuers of the more earnest Protestāts, whose intentions therein (supposing their Religion were true) are most commendable. I here may be the more bould to rest in such examples (I hope) without offence to any Protestant Reader (which willingly I labour to auoyde,) because they are warranted by the Protestants owne practise, though in a different Religion. Therefore their actiōs for the aduancement of their Religion, may be a spur and incitement to vs, to practise the like actions for the Honour of our Catholike Religion,

Reddes nouissimum

gion, which is most Ancient and infallible.

For no small dishonour it would be to vs Catholikes, that those words of sacred writ should be auerred herein of them and vs: *Filij huius saeculi prudentiores filijs lucis in sua generatione sunt.Luc.16. The children of this world are more wise in their generation, then the Children of light.* For shall such men, whose Fayth euen depreiseth the merit of *Good Workes*, exceed the Catholikes in the practise of their supposed *Good Workes?* O no. Let therfore our owne practize of *Good Workes* become a *Scholia*, to paraphraze our doctrine, & beliefe touching *Good Workes*. And how preposterous would it be, that our Aduersaries putting no confidence in *Good Works*, should neuerthelesse in their owne iudgments be ready to performe them? We, who put confidence in them, as receauing their worth from the Merits of Christ his Passion, and his promisse of reward to them (& not otherwise) yet should be slow in the operation of them? Therfore may we not blush, that our owne cold remissnes in good actions, should become

Reddes nouissimum

against Purgatory.

a foyle to their greater seeming Actions of that Nature?

Well then, to descend to particulars: We obserue, that the more forward Protestants, fynding Youths (though meere strangers vnto them) of pregnancy and hope to be Schollars, will strayne themselnes & open their purses, to maintayne them in our english Vniuersities; that finally they may become Ministers, thereby more & more to disseminate in the Realme their owne Protestant Religion. Now seeing the Catholike Religion

quadrantem.

gion is only true, for *Vna fides, vnum Baptisma, Ephes.* 4. how meritorious and pleasing is it in the sight of God, for you to practize the like Charity to yōg poore schollars of hopefull expectation, for their bringing vp in such places of literature, as that when they haue ended their studies, they may be seruiceable in the Catholike Church for the general good of others?

I instance (for example) in a pregnant yong boy of seauenteene, or eighteene yeares of age; This boy through want of meanes, for

Reddes nouissimum his

against Purgatory.

his better preferment is to become a Seruingman, a Clarke, a Prentise, or at the best (indeed the worst) a Minister; In all which states, considering the present streme of Protestancy in England, his soule is in all likelyhood to perish eternally, for his not dying in a true Fayth, and Religion. Now here obserue the wonderfull difference, rising from the performing, or omitting of such a charitable deed. Yf such a boy stay in England, then is his soule (as aboue is said) in great perill of eternally perishing, through his

quadrantem.

professing of an erroneous Fayth: Yf he be Catholikly brought vp, and sent ouer the sea's, he is to be instructed in the only sauing Catholike Faith, to the most hopefull Saluation of his soule.

Yf he be here sent to our English Vniuersities, and finally become a Minister; he then, not only looseth his owne soule, but is to be feared, will be the cause of the euerlasting perdition of many other mens Soules, by his enuenoming, and infecting their Iudgments with his owne Religion: Yf he be brought vp in Catholike

Reddes uouissimum.

pla-

places, beyond the Seas, and proceed forward in his courfe, he then (liuing according to the ſtrict courſe of his vndertaken Profeſſion,) not only ſaueth his owne Soule, but is a ſubordinate Inſtrument vnder God, for the ſauing of many other mens ſoules; partly by practiſing his function among ſuch as be already Catholikes; and partly by his perſuaſion (if ſo he proue learned,) of others yet remaining Proteſtants, to imbrace the Roman Catholike Fayth.

And thus if you obſerue,

either the preuenting of the great Hurt, and *Euill*, which is in likely-hood to come by the youthes taking the one course of life; or the great *Spirituall good* to himselfe & others, by his vndergoing the other State: You may thinke your siluer employed to such an Act, to be most happily layed out; Assuring your selues, that the worke of the *Euill* here preuented, and the *Good* here performed (& all originally vnder *God*, by your meanes) shall find a great retaliation at Gods most mercifull hands, both for the increase of your me-

Reddes nouissimum rits,

against Purgatory.

rits, as also for the expiating of your sinnes, which otherwise is to be performed in *Purgatory.*

Why then therfore should such of you, as be of the greater Ranke and best abilities, be slow in practizing workes of this nature? Therfore now, while you haue tyme, lay wayte by all conuenient meanes to enquyre after such occasions; Especially when such a particular worthy Act may oftentymes be performed with lesser charges, then diuers of you wil bestow vpon a good suite of apparel. O thē, apparaile and inuest your Soules with such good workes; and be lesse chargeable in gorgeous attire for your bodies. I do assure you, if I had great and abūdant meanes for the practizing of the workes of Piety, I had rather make choyce to distribute to this vse of prouiding and maintaining of hopeful youths in learning, to the end aboue expressed, then to any other particular End whatsoeuer. For if neither any places of Residence beyond the Seas had beene prouided, and furnished with sufficient maintenance for the bringing vp

Reddes nouissimum of

of English Schollers; nor that there had beene any Catholikes, who would haue opened their purses to this noble End, Catholike Religion had beene vtterly extinct many yeares since, in England.

This Zeale of many good Catholikes both dead (and no doubt, aliue) in this point, is the fuell, that hath nourished, and kept in, the fyer of Catholike Religion in our owne Country for many yeares past. Since if Youths were not sent ouer to be (after their studies ended) created Priestes, how

quadrantem. Math. 5.

could the profession of Catholike Religion continue in these so great stormes among vs? Therefore what a great and inexplicable comfort will it be to you in your last Sicknes, euen for satisfaction of your temporall punishments, when you shall remember, that wheras such, or such a pregnant youth was in the high way of perdition, and of ouerthrowing his owne, and other mens soules also, if he had proceeded in his former intended Course of life; yet you (through your charity) in laying out a little peece of

Reddes nouissimum

money, did vnder God, therby rescue the sayd youth, euen out of the Deuills iawes, and haue beene a second meanes of sauing both the youths owne soule, & of the soules of diuers others?

This being so, let me then intreat you (*Most worthy Catholikes*) euen for our Sauiours sake (who gaue not siluer (as is heere only expected) but his most precious bloud, for the ransoning of all soules out of the Deuills possession.) that you would cast a most serious, and intense consideration of this one point. And thus far tou-

quadrantem. Math. 5.   ching

ching this particular kind of Almes-deeds.

Only this much more I will annex, as an *Appendix* to the former, that I could wish the most able of you in temporall state, to haue a feeling and sensible touch of diuers well-disposed yonge gentlewomen; who through the decay of their Parents state, not hauing sufficient portions left them to enter into Religion (being of themselues otherwise most desirous to shake handes for euer with the world, by taking that course) are forced to forbeare that their most

Reddes nouissimum Re-

Religious inclination, & for want of meanes to take some secular Course of life, either by mariage, or otherwise.

Now here, how truly Worthy and Heroicall a part of Christian Catholike Munificene and bounty were it in you, by increasing their Portions, to supply such their wants, & thereby to turne the channell of their otherwise dágerous courses Which if you do performe, what haue you done? This you haue done. You haue caused a yong Gentle-woman (otherwise exposed, & lying open to the dangers of the

quadrantem. Math. 5. world)

world) to Cloyster herselfe within a wall, there to spēd all her lyfe tyme, in Chasti-ty, Obedience, Voluntary pouerty, and other deuotiōs; rysing at midnight (to forbeare all other her austerities) when your selues are taking your sweet repose & rest, to sing laudes to God, & to pray for her benefactours, & particularly for you, who haue beene the cause of such her most happy choyce of life: she thus by your charity increasing the number of those, *qui sequuntur agnum; quocumque ierit. Apoc.* 14. Here is an Act deseruing the

---
Reddes nouissimum true

true name of Christian charity, and such as shalbe able (through Gods most mercifull acceptance therof) to arme the Soule against the Flames of *Purgatory*.

But to proceed to other sorts of good Deeds, practised by the forward Protestant. We see in most places of the Realme, that there are diuers earnest Protestants, who seeing some neighboring places wanting preaching Ministers, are ready to plant such men there; affording them large allowáce, & this to the end, the more to dilate their owne Protestan-

---
quadrantem. Math. 5.

ticall Fayth, ouer much allready spread and disseminated. And hence it is, that so many Stipendary Ministers are setled in seuerall places of the Realme. Now, why should such of you as be of greater ability, be inferiour in Zeale to the Protestants herein, as to suffer such vacant places, as are neare to you, to be destitute of all such Instruments in the Catholike Faith? I doubt not but that diuers of you, seeing a peece of land close by you, though rough and vntilled; yet of it owne Nature (through smal charges) most

Reddes nouissimum fruit-

fruitfull: I doubt not (I say) but that diuers of you would be desirous, either to buy, or at least to take a Lease of the said land, therby to better your states the more. There are diuers wast places adioyning to euery one of you, wherein liue many ciuill & morall men, yet their vnderstanding (in regard of any Religion) are but as *Tabulæ Rasæ*, or vnmanured land.

Now heere, what a most worthy and Christian attempt, and endeauour were it in you, to seeke to plant spirituall labourers in such places, by whose paynes the

quadrantem. Math. 5:

seed of Catholike Religion might be sowne in mens soules; since the *Georgikes* of the mind (so to speake) are far more worthy & noble, then the *Georgikes* or Agriculature of land? And would not then those sacred textes of Scripture here be verified of you: *Seminanti iustitiam merces fidelis*, Prou. 11. He that soweth righteousnes, receaueth a sure reward: and againe: *Qui operatur terram suam, inaltabit aceruum frugum*, Eccl. 20. Who tilleth his land, shall increase his heape of Corne; to wit Heauenly Corne?

O what a spirituall in-

Reddes nouissimum creafe

creale might such of you make, who haue full and open purses, by cultiuating of diuers of these barrē places? And how forcible would such pious endeuours be, for the expiating of the relicks of your sinnes? Therefore let not the Puritan Gentilmen, and others, exceed and ouergoe you in their Zeale towards God (though *Zeale not according to knowledg. Rom. 10.*) in this point, who are most liberall in maintaining of their Preachers, and all to plant their Errours, to the spirituall Danger of the soules of their credulous and ignorant

quadrantem. Math. 5.

norant Hearers; But labour by secret meanes without contestation to the present state (to which you ought euer to beare all duty and reuerence) to supererogate with them, in pious workes of this Nature.

An other point, wherein we may well follow the steps of our Aduersaries, is this. The Protestant Gentlemen (though of very great worth and Ranke) do often send their yonger Sonnes to our English Vniuersities, prouiding that they may become fellowes of Houses; whose *Terminus ad quem* (as I

Reddes noniſſimum may

against Purgatory.

may say) is finally to become Ministers, and thereby to be promoted to great and rich Ecclesiasticall liuings; in which store and abundance, *England* exceedeth all Nations in Christendome. Now to be emulous of our Aduersaries proceeding herein: if Catholike Parents would seriously ponder this point, no doubt they would be more carefull and willing to send ouer their yonger sonnes to Catholike Colledges beyond the Seas, then they are; not to become schollars, only thereby to be aduanced to spirituall liuings (an ouer vnworthy Allectiue) but to become Priests, (that throgh sheeding of their bloud) euen after an Apostolicall manner, they may labour to reduce their owne Country to its former ancient Catholike and Roman Fayth.

Now, such yonger Brothers of Catholikes, which haue not their education abroad, but only bred vp in England; into what (for the most part) do they finally resolue? They (for example) being left by their Parents Twenty, or Thirty, or perhaps forty pounds Annuity (and sometimes lesse then,

Reddes nouissimum any

any of these) what course do most of these after their parents decease, vsually vndergoe? To be in seruice to any mā or Knight or Nobleman of worth, or to be in any good employment abroad for their temporall aduancement, many of them out of a long habituated idlenes, and as being at their owne disposall and liberty, will not. And what then commonly do they? Forsooth they rest content with their owne poore Annuities, burdening commonly their Elder Brother (if he be a man of a good and kind Nature) for their diet; and they rauell out their yeares, walking vp and downe, and domineiring among their Eldest Brothers Tenants and Neighbours, with a Marlin, or Sparhauke on their fist, & a Grey-hound, or water spanell following them (the very badge, or armes of most yonger Brothers in diuers Shyres) hiding themselues for the most part of the day, in some base Ale-house; and often becomming (through dissolution of life) Fathers, before they be Husbands. But in the end (belike for feare their House, from

Reddes nouissimum whence

whence they descend, should be extinct for wāt of Heires) they marry their Sister-in-lawes wayting mayde, or some other poore woman, and then they beget a litter of Beggars, both burdensome, and dishonorable to their Family and Stock.

But now, if we cast our eye vpon the other end of the ballance: Yf such yonger sonnes of Catholike Parēts (being of good wits) were sent ouer in their Parents life time, and that when their minds and wills were of a supple and waxen Disposition, as not being acquainted afore (through want of yeares) with any sinne or Euill, and ready to receaue the impression of Vertue & learning; how seruiceable to the Church of God in tyme, might such men become? For by this meanes of education, many of them do vndergoe (as we fynd by experience) a most holy Function of life; spending their whole age after, in laboring to administer the Sacraméts of the Church to Catholikes, in reducing diuers Protestants to the only true and Catholike Fayth, and in daily praying & offering vp the most Venerable

Reddes nouissimum Sa-

Sacrifice of Christes body, for the soules of their dead Parents, and others their liuing or deceased Friends. *O quantum distat ortus ab occasu?* for so great is the Disparity betweene these two differet courses of Yonger Brothers here set downe; not only in the eye of God, but euen in the eye of the world.

And heere by digression I will touch a little vpon the Daughters of Catholicke Gentle-men. Heere in *England* diuers of them (as well as the Daughters of Protestants) take (throgh a blind affection, often cast vpō some base man or other) a most vnworthy Course, to the vnutterable griefe of their Parents, and ouerthrow of their temporall state. And if they be placed in mariage with their Parents consent answerably to their Degree; yet if either the Husbands proue vnkind, or in course of life vitious; or their Children vntoward and licentious, what a vexation is it then to the Parents? And how do they languishingly spend their dayes in inconsolable sighs and sorrow?

But now, if the said Daughters, being in their

Reddes nouissimum Vir-

against Purgatory.

Virginall, tender, and innocent age, be brought vp in places of Religion, and that through the speciall grace of God, and meanes of ther daily education, they proceed and become Religious women in the Church of God; How ineffable a comfort may this be to their Catholike parents? Since they then by these meanes, freeing theselues from all illaqueations and worldly entanglements, shall bestow the greatest part both of Day and Night in performing, & singing Hymnes of Prayses to his Diuine Maiesty, for the

quadrantem.

good of themselues & their Friends: To euery one of which, at the Close of their lyfe may be said in the Catholicke Churches *Dialect: Veni sponsa Christi, accipe coronam, quam tibi Dominus præparauit in æternum.* (*in Collect. Natalit. Virg.*

Thus far of this point. And I would to God, that Catholicke Parents would apprehend this Paragraph or passage with a serious & feeling consideration. And thus far of these former Courses, in imitating the examples of our Aduersaries; which exāples were most worthy of

Reddes nouissimum all

against Purgatory.

all commendation, being incorporated in an Orthodoxall Religion. But yet heere, in our Imitation of them, I euer wish, that what is attempted in this kind (or els not to be attempted) were performed (as before I intimated) with all sweetnes, and moderation, and with all dutifull Respect to the state of our Realme. Since I hould it most repugnant to true Iudgment & Religion, to vndertake to put in practise orderly things, by vnorderly meanes; and therefore in all such our spirituall endeauours let vs remember, to shew all duty and reuerence to the State, and that it is recorded in sacred Writ, (*Rom.* 13.) *We are to be subiect to higher powers; seeing there is no power, but of God.* And there againe: *Who resisteth the Power, resisteth the Ordinance of God.* In regard of which promptnes of our duty, I hope thofe examples, as being taken by imitation from the Proteſtants themſelues, will not be iuſtly offenſiue to the graue Proteſtant Magiſtrate.

    There is yet another thing most worthy of your charitable commiſeration. You

---

Reddes noniſſimum   ſee,

see, that the Catholickes throughout England pay yerely great sommes of money for their Recusancy; Among whom, there are many hundred of poore Catholikes, who are so ouercharged with these yearely payments, as that their meane Estates are not able to support any long time such payments; of which his Maiesty (who is most prone to commiseration and pitty) litle heareth in particular; this being effected only by certaine Subordinate Magistrates, aduerse to our Catholike Religion. And thereupon

quadrantem. Math. 5.

for their auoiding of the said payments, imposed vpon them, diuers of these poore men and women haue forsaken already (contrary to their conscience) externally their Religion, and are content to come to the Protestant Church.

Now heere I say, such of you, as be of great Abilities, how ample a field haue you to sow your merits and satisfactions in; I meane by contributing out of your purses some yearly sommes to these poore Catholikes, thereby to ease, and lessen their yearely payments? In

Reddes nouissimum your

against Purgatory.

your worthy performāce of this my propounded Motion, you do not only help and succour them touching their bodies; but (which is far more pleasing in the sight of God,) you so take pitty of their soules, as you preuent, that diuers of them do not Apostatate & forsake their Catholicke Religion, which perhaps throgh feare of want of meanes they would doe; And so you are become a secondary great Instrument of their finall Saluation.

And can you then otherwise thinke, but that God

quadrantem. Math.5. (who

(who is mercy it selfe) and who will take this Charity of yours as done to himselfe, would take the like pitty of your owne soules, both for the preuenting of your eternall perdition, as also for mitigating your temporall punishments in Purgatory? For heer our Sauiours words would be iustified in you, *Math.* 25. *Verily I say vnto you; In so much as you haue donne it vnto one of the least of these my brethren, you haue done it vnto me.*

In this next place, I will descend to acts peculiar onely to vs Catholikes; & such as do insist, and rest in offering vp the prayers both of our selues, but especially of the generall Liturgy of the most blessed Sacrifice of the Eucharist, offered vp either for the benefit of our selues, or of others. Of which most dreadfull Sacrifice sayth *S. Chrysostome homil. 25. in Act. Apost. Hostia in manibus, adsunt Angeli, adsunt Archangeli, adest Filius Dei, cum tanto horrore astant omnes.* And to begin; Thinke what a worthy, and charitable Act it were to concurre by causing Sacrifices and Prayers to be made, for the redeeming of

quadrantem. Math. 5. poore

poore Soules out of *Purgatory*

There is no man of an Humane and sweet Nature, but he would commiserate a very beast (much more a man) lying in extremity of paynes. And this Naturall Pitty is so gratefull to our Sauiour himselfe, as that he pronounceth, *Matth. 5. Beati misericordes, quoniam ipsi misericordiam consequentur; Blessed are the mercifull, for they shall obtayne mercy:* So auaylable & behooffull is pitty and mercy to the performers thereof. But to proceed to another benefit of such a pious deed.

Reddes novissimum

Yf a prudent man, had a Cause of most great importance, to be tryed before a seuere, yet most iust Iudge; And if at the same tyme, there were certaine persons in prison, whom that Iudge did much respect, & to whose earnest solicitations in any reasonable point, he would lend a willing eare: Now would not this Suppliant lay wayte by all meanes to redeeme the said men out of Prison, if so he could (who during their stay there, were put to daily torments and rackings) as well assuring himselfe, that these Persons

quadrantem. Math. 5.

thus set at liberty by this mans meanes (being men of most good and gratefull Natures & Dispositions) would be ready to speake to the Iudge, and be earnest and solicitous in his behalfe? And then is it not most probable (if not certaine) that this man would speed the better in determining his Cause?

The case is here a like, and both are cast (as it were) in one mould. The soules in *Purgatory* (once from thence released) shall become most blessed Saints in Heauen, & shall be most pleasing and gratefull to his Diuine Ma-

Reddes nouissimum iesty;

iesty; who cannot, nor will not deny them the grant of any thing, which they shall demaund, and petition for at his hands.

Euery Catholike (as all other men) are to plead their cause before God, the most iust Iudge: Yet for the more easy obtayning of their Plea, it is in the power of ech Catholike of good meanes (if his will be answerable thereto) to procure, at least much to further, by his liberall charges bestowed for the praying for the soules in *Purgatory*, the releasing and setting free of diuers of the

quadrantem. Math.5. said

said tormented soules.

Now this being once performed, those then Happy Soules, shall no sooner leaue their Goale and Prison, and ascend to Heauen; but as euen abounding with a Seraphicall Charity, shall in recompéce of so great a spirituall ease and Relaxation procured to them, euer batter at the eares of our Almighty and mercifull Lord, with their daily and incessant prayers; that his Diuine Mercy would be most indulgent and pittifull to such men, for the preuenting (or at least mitigating) of their

Reddes nouissimum tem-

temporall paynes, by whose meanes those soules had a more speedy deliuery from their torments in *Purgatory*.

Heere then may a man, who is rich in temporall state (if so he be rich in charity) lay out his wealth to an infinite increase of spirituall gayne. O how many peculiar *Aduocates* and *Intercessours* of the then most blessed soules (released out of *Purgatory*) might a rich Catholike purchase to himselfe, by this former meanes, thereby to pleade his cause before the Throne of Almighty God, in his greatest need?

---

quadrantem. Math.5.

need? And fooles (I will not say Madmen) are all such, vpon whom God hath bestowed abundance of temporall riches; and yet themselues remayne vnwilling & slow in this spirituall traffique of a good and competent part of their said temporall state and meanes.

But because this point of relieuing by *Good Workes* the soules in *Purgatory*, is of most great importance, both to the poore soules relieued, & the liuing party performing such a most charitable work to them: Therefore besydes what is already deliuered

---

Reddes nouissimum by

by me aboue, I will adioyne (as most mouing any man of Piety and Iudgment) the discourse of the aforementioned learned and worthy *Cardinall Bellarmine* of this point; who maketh the ninth Chapter of the third booke *de Gemitu Columba*, the subiect hereof: Thus then that blessed man writeth: *We haue shewed aboue, that there are very many, or rather innumerable soules of the faithfull in Purgatory; and that they are a most long tyme to be tormented, almost with increaible punishments. Now here we will declare the fruite, which may be* gathered from this consideration. And certainly it cannot be doubted, but if the ponderation and weighing of this point be serious, longe, attent, and full of fayth and confidence; a most vehement commiseration, and full of horrour and feare will result out of the said consideration.

And in like sort it is certaine, that an earnest and intense consideration of the said point, will engender in vs a vehement desire of helping the said soules in Purgatory, by satisfactory workes; to wit, Prayer, Fasting, Almes-deeds, and chiefly by the most holy oblation, and Sacrifice

Reddes nouißimum

of our Lords body. And indeed it is most admirable to obserue, how gainfull a negotiation (and this most iust) may accrew vnto vs thereby. And this spirituall negotiation may well be resambled to the proceeding of a man, who should deliuer one and the same siluer (vpon vsury) to seuerall Merchants; and yet should receaue a full and entyre Interest for one and the said Siluer, from euery one of the Merchants.

Let vs explayne our selues in few words. A man prayeth for the Dead, attentiuely, piously, with fayth, and great confidence of impetratiou and obtaining the thing prayed for. This man so praying, by way of merit purchaseth to himselfe the gayne of eternall felicity and happines: since Prayer is a good worke, & in that respect deseruing eternall life, if it proceed from Charity. Of which gayne our Lord speaketh in the Ghospell in these words, *Matth. 6. Tu autem cum oraueris &c.* Thou, when thou shalt pray, enter into thy chamber, and hauing shut the doore, pray to thy Father in secret; and thy Father; who seeth thee in secret, will repay thee; To wit, a Reward answerable to the merit.

Furthermore, this praying

Reddes nouissimum for

*for the Dead, by way of satisfa-
ction, doth profit the departed
soule in Purgatory, for the which
it is performed: seeing Prayer is
(amongst others) a laborious
worke, and therein it is satisfactory; and consequently it is profitable for that soule, to which it
is applyed, according to the in-
tention of him that prayeth, &
the Doctrine of the Church. To
conclude by way of impetration
and humbly begging, it profiteth
the said departed soule, whose
freeing from Purgatory, at least
whose ease and mitigation of
those paynes, is therin beseeched
and desired. Since that, for
which Iust men pray to God,*
quadrantem.   *through*

through Christ, is eastly obtayned: Our Lord himselfe saying Luc. 11. *Petite, & accipietis &c.* Aske, and you shall receaue, and againe, Matt. 11. *Quicquid orantes, petitis &c.* All things whatsoeuer you aske, praying, belieue that you shall receaue, and they shall come vnto you. And more, Ioan. 16. *Si quid petieritis &c.* If you aske the Father any thing in my name, he shall giue it you.

Behould heere a threefould gayne, proceeding from prayer, made in behalfe of the soules departed. But there may be aduowed a fourth benefit: That is, the soules, for which we pray,

Reddes nouissimum will

will not be vngratefull, when they shall arriue into their heauenly Country; but shall answere & recompence our prayers, with their like prayers in our behalfe.

To proceed; Fasting being performed by vs, and applyed for the deceased, obtayneth a manifould gaine. For first, (as a meritorious worke) it is profitable to him, who fasteth, euen by the testimony of our Lord himselfe Matth. 6. Tu autem, cum ieiunas, &c. When thou dost fast, annoynt thy head, and wash thy face, that thou appeare not to men to fast, but to thy Father, which is in secret; and thy Fa-

quadrantem.

ther, which seeth in secret, will repay thee.

Fasting also, as a satisfactory worke, being applyed for the dead, doth helpe the dead. For not without iust cause, did David fast, with all his retinue and trayne euen till night, when he was aduertized of the ouerthrow of King Saul, and Ionathas, and of a great part of the people of God.

To conclude, Fasting (in an other manner) profiteth the party so fasting; to wit, in that the soules of the departed, when they shall ascend to Heauen, will not be forgetfull of their Benefactours; but will power out prayers

Reddes nouissimum

against Purgatory. 249

for them; and such their prayers, as proceeding from true Charity, shall be heard.

Now, in this next place, to come to *Almes-deeds.* This kind of good Worke also is accompanied with a threefould gayne. For first, it profiteth the poore, to which the *Almes-deeds* are giuen, and maketh them to become our friends, that so when we fayle, they may receaue vs into eternall *Tabernacles. Luc.*16. Againe, *Almes-deeds* being applyed for the vse of the soules departed, do bring a refreshing and refocillation to the said soules; and consequently make them also to become our friends,

quadrantem.   L 5   Who

who hauing a title to the Kingdome of Heauen, will no doubt helpe vs with their holy Prayers and Intercessions.

Thirdly, Almes-deeds do (as I may say) bynd God to be a debtour vnto vs; for thus the Holy Ghost speaketh by the mouth of Salomon: *Qui miseretur pauperis, fœneratur Domino*: Who taketh pitty of the poore, doth put out his siluer to interest, euen to our Lord. *Prou.* 19. And Christ confirmeth the same in the Gospell, saying, *Matth.* 6. *Te faciente Eleemosynam &c.* When thou dost an Almes deed, let not thy left hand know, what thy right hand doth, that thy Almes-

Reddes nouissimum deed

deed may be secret, and thy Father, which seeth in secret, will repay thee.

To descend to the most blessed Sacrifice of Christs body & bloud; It is most cleare and euident, that that oblation profiteth the party, who offereth it vp, as a guift most gratefull to God: It profiteth the faithfull liuing, as also the faithfull soules departed. And that this is most vndoubtedly true, appeareth from the many most credible Visions or apparitions, manifesting that the faithfull soules in Purgatory, do desire and expect nothing more, then that the most celestiall oblation of the body and

bloud of Christ may be offered
vp for their refreshing, or freeing them from their paynes. Of
which point read S. Gregory lib.
4. Dialogorum. cap. 75. & se-
quent. Also the History of England writen by Venerable Bede
lib. 5. cap. 13.

In like sort the Epistles of
Petrus Damianus ad Deside-
rium, may be read; & finally the
lyfe of S. Nicolaus Tolentinus
in Surius tom. 5. ad diem 10.
Septembris: For to this blessed
Priest appeared once a great
multitude of soules, who with
teares and most lachrimall voy-
ces desired of him the celebration
of the most holy Sacrifice, as a

Reddes novissimum

against Purgatory. 253

principall Remedy for their paines in Purgatory. Now from all the Premisses, it is euident, that we may receaue a most preciable and incomparable gayne, if we daily powre out our prayers, for the soules departed; or if we do distribute Almes to the poore, for the ease and refreshment of their paynes; or if we do satisfy for the said soules, either by our Fasting, or other penitential works; or finally do celebrate the most holy Sacrifice of the Masse for their deliuery out of Purgatory. Thus far learned *Bellarmine* discourseth of this point: Whose words I would desire euery good Catholicke

---
quadrantem. Math. 5.   Rea-

Reader seriously to obserue.

But to enlarge my selfe a little further, I could wish all of you of good states, when iust occasiõ is presented, that you would be most bountifull in relieuing imprisoned Priests, and poore imprisoned Catholiks. O how worthy an Act is this, and how do you suffer in their sufferings? And you may then infallibly interest your selues in the words of the Apostle, *Hebr.* 6. *God is not vniust, that he can forget your good workes, and charity, which you haue shewed in his name, and haue, and do minister vnto*

Reddes nouissimum   his

against Purgatory. 255

his Saints.

 I well remember, that some twenty yeares since, a certaine Prison hauing in it some six or seauen Priests, & far more poore lay Catholikes, lying there in great want; there was a Catholike gentle-woman of good account, who taking great comiseration of their wants, relieued all the Catholike imprisoned company, with weekly prouision of meate for seuerall months; and so she intended still to continue this her Charity, but that she was shortly after preuented by death. This was

quadrantem. Matth. 5.   an

an Heroicall and most Christian charity in her, able no doubt (throgh Christs mercifull acceptance thereof) euen to abate the flames of *Purgatory.*

In like sort, I could wish all of you, who are carefull to preuent the raging flames of *Purgatory*, that what workes of labour, or satisfaction, or Almes deeds you inted to doe, that you would not defer the accomplishing of them, till the day of your departure out of this world; but performe them when you are in health. The difference is most great betweene

Reddes nouissimum

a worke of Charity done at the Houre of a mans death, and when he is in health not likely to dye.

For in the first manner, the party dying, giueth away his goods to pious vses, because he cannot enioy them any longer. In the second, it is in a mans power to keep his riches longer, & yet departing from them in his Health, he is content thereby actually to lessen in his owne daies his temporall meanes, and departeth with them with cherefulnes and alacrity of mind; a circumstance most pleasing to God,

quadrantem. Math. 5. since

since we read) 2. *Cor.* 9. *Hilarem datorem diligit Deus*; *God loueth a chearfull giuer.* In the former, the will of a dying man is not (for the most part) in all things performed, either through the Couetousnes of the wife, Children, or negligence of the Executors: In this other, a man is assured his will shall be performed; since he is resolued to make his owne *Hands*, his *Executors*, and his owne *Eyes*, his *Ouerseers.*

Lastly, Almes-deeds done after the first sort, do take effect only at the death of the Party & not before; whereas they being distributed after this second sort, they begin to worke and obtaine by degrees Indulgéce, lesseuing of the future paynes, euen from that houre, in which they were first bestowed: So great a disparity there is betweene hauing a Candell going before a man, lighting him the way to the Kingdome of Heauen, & hauing a Candell only to follow him.

I am persuaded, there are very few of you so simple, who if you did owe great summes of Money, and were infallibly to pay euery penny of them, if other courfe

quadrantem. Math. 5.

in the meane tyme could not be taken; But that if by preuention of time (I meane by paying afore the day of payment cōmeth) you might be suffered in lieu of the whole, to pay but the twentith part, and thereby to be discharged of the whole great debt; but that you would take course by all meanes possible (yea by taking your siluer vp at Interest) for the present discharge of the said twentith part, so to redeeme your selues from the payment of all the rest. I do assure you euen from the testimonies of all

Reddes nouissimum an-

ancient & learned Fathers, that it is in your power to redeeme not only the twentith part of your future torments in Purgatory, but euen the greatest part, and perhaps all, by your charitable Deeds, liberality, and pious workes, now done in your life time: And will you then be slow in taking the like course herein? *O insensati Galata, quis vos fascinauit? Gal. 3.* But I will yet go further with you.

There are not many of you (I speake of such of you as are much deuoted to the world) but that, if you had

quadrantem. Math. 5.

a fayre demayne of fiue hundred pounds yearely worth, though not in possession; yet that it were infallibly to descend to you and your Posterity for euer, after twenty yeares were expired; And that notwithstáding it were in your Power & Freedome, to buy out and redeeme the said twenty yeares, thereby to haue present possession of it; I say, there are not many of you, but that you would striue, though it were by impouerishing your selues for the tyme, and by liuing vnder your owne worth, thereby to procure meanes

Reddes nouissimum for

for the redeeming of the said terme of twenty yeares.

Heauen is your Inheritance, after the guilt of eternall damnation is once remitted; Yet thither it is impossible for you to arriue, vntil for certaine yeares you haue performed your temporall punishments yet remaining. These inexplicable punishments, which may endure for many scores of yeares, more then twenty, (yea it may be for seuerall hundreds of yeares) you may redeeme perhaps for lesse charges to your Purse, disbursed in your life time and

quadrantem Math.5.

health to pious & religious vses (through Chrifts moſt mercifull acceptance,) then you would be content to lay out, for the getting in of the former mentioned twenty yeares. And yet how Dull, and Backward are moſt of you to vndertake the fame? How can you heere Apologize or excufe your felues? Is Heauen not fo good, as an earthly demaine? O men of little Fayth! What a muddy difpofition of the Soule is this, which lyes fo groueling vpon the earth, and wholy abforpt in terrene thoughts and cogitations?

Reddes noviſſimum   Well

Well, ceasing to enlarge my selfe further vpon the Premisses, I earnestly desire euery one of you, to procure now in tyme of Health, the most Reuerend & Dreadfull Sacrifice of the most blessed body and bloud of our Sauiour to be offered daily vp, to two ends; to wit, for the spirituall good of your selues and your Children; and secondly, for the preuenting of your future paines of *Purgatory*. And that you shall perceaue of what ineffable vertue and efficacy for mans soule, the offering vp of that most dreadfull Sacrifice is, I

haue

haue thought good to set downe the Iudgmentes of some few ancient Fathers, pretermitting the greatest part of them, for greater breuity.

First then we find *S. Cyrill of Alexandria Epist. ad Nestor.* to write, that by meanes of this daily Sacrifice, *We are made partakers of the holy body and precious bloud of Christ. S. Austin* calleth the said Sacrifice, *Precium nostrum*, *Our pryce. Confess. cap.* 13. And further the same Father thus writeth *lib. 4. de Trinit. cap.* 14. *Quid gratius offerri &c. What can be offered vp, or accepted*

Reddes nouissimum   more

more thankefully, then that the flesh of our Sacrifice, should become the body of our Priest?

S. Chrysostome thus teacheth, *Homil.* 21. *in Act. Apostolorum. Hostia in manibus &c.* The sacred host being in the hands of the Priest, the Angels are present, the Archangels are present, the sonne of God is present, *cum tanto horrore astant omnes*, with so much feare and horrour all of them are present. S. Gregory Nyssene thus expresly writeth, *Orat. Catech. c.* 36. *Fidelium corporibus &c.* That body (meaning the body of Christ in the Sacrifice of the Masse) is ioyned with the bodies of the faythfull, that by the coniunction of the immortall body, man may be made partaker of immortality. S. *Cyprian* thus teacheth of the offering vp of the body, and bloud of Christ in the holy Eucharist (*Serm. de cœna Dom.*) *Perpes est hoc sacrificium &c.* This is a daily Sacrifice, and is a permanent or perpetuall Holocaust. To conclude the foremétioned S. *Chrysostome* thus writeth (*hom. 2. in 1. ad Cor.*) *Dum in hac vita sumus &c.* Whiles we are in this life, this mistery of the Eucharist maketh, that the earth it selfe, is a Heauen to vs.

Reddes nouissimum   And

And now hauing shewed out of the testimonies of the ancient Fathers, the impreciable efficacy and vertue of the most Reuerend Sacrifice of Christs body and bloud, for the spirituall good of mans Soule; we may from thence conclude, that the daily offering vp of the said most dreadfull Sacrifice (cōsidering the worth of him there sacrificed) is most auaylable & behoofull, both for the soules of men yet liuing, thereby to arme and strengthen them with grace, against all the temptations of the World and the diuell, as also for the expiating of mans Sinnes in *Purgatory*. Sweet Iesus! no other impetration, or prayer is more piercing in the eares of God, then this; since heere (for remitting of our sinnes, and regulating our actions for the tyme hereafter with diuine grace) the *Sonne* pleadeth to the *Father*, *God* to *God*; And the same man, is both the *Priest*, and the *Sacrifice*.

Yea this most Reuerend Mystery of the Sacrifice of the *Masse*, is the very center of Religion, and hart of deuotion; by meanes whereof

Reddes nouissimum

his diuine Maiesty most bountifully imparteth, and powreth out his fauours and graces to our soules: So certaine and infallible it is, that our Prayers made in Vnion of this diuine Sacrifice (whether for our spirituall good during our Peregrination in this world, or for the taking away of the paines of *Purgatory*,) haue an inexplicable power and efficacy: And therfore those men are great Enemies to themselues, and their Children, who neglect this so soueraigne a meanes, both for their owne & their Childrens aduancement in sanctity and Vertue.

Yet before I end this discourse, I must adioyne this ensuing Animaduersion; that whereas most of the former examples of *Good Workes* aboue alledged, & instanced, aime at great & high points; sorting only to such to performe, whose temporall states are great and rich, and to whom that admonition of *S. Chrysostome* (aboue alledged) peculiarly belongeth, *Non dare, sed copiosè dare Eleemosyna est*: Neuerthelesse we are to conceaue, that the Charity of such, as be but poore in temporall faculties

Reddes nouissimum though

though, neuer so small, are most pleasing to his diuine Maiesty, for the mitigating of the torments of *Purgatory.* And in this sense we must vnderstand, that euen the poore *Widdow* in the Ghospell, who had but two mites, gaue as much as *Zachæus,* who contributed the halfe of his great substance to the poore; because, though the widdow had lesser goods to giue, yet she had the like will of giuing; And though, that which was seuerally giuen by them both, were vnequall & diuers; yet the fountaine from whence they gaue (to

---

quadrantem. Math. 5. wit

wit from a prompt and charitable disposition of relieuing the poore) was the same. And thus did it fall out, that whereas the whole *Widowes* state was but small, yet the part thereof giuen, was great; *Since he giueth no litle, who freely and cheerefully giueth a part of a little.* And therefore the foresaid *S. Chrysostome* accordingly thus teacheth (*Hom.* 34. *ad pop. Antioch.*) *Eleemosinæ magnitudo, non in pecuniarum multitudine iudicatur, sed in dantiũ promptitudine.* With whom accordeth *S. Leo* (*ser.* 4. *de Quadrag.*) saying, *Ex affecti-*

Reddes nouissimum   *bus*

bus piorum, benignitatis mensura taxatur.

Well, I will close vp this small Treatise with referring the Catholicke Reader, to the practise of a skillfull Phisitian, who can extract medicinable and healthfull Physick, out of hurtfull and venemous drugs or hearbs: So heere I most earnestly wish, that all good Catholikes (according to the different proportion of their states and power) would in their owne life time (for the preuenting or lessening of the torments of *Purgatory*) put in daily practise that *quadrantem. Math. 5.* coun-

counsell of our Sauiour:
Luc. 16. *Facite vobis amicos de Mammona iniquitatis, vt cum defeceritis, recipiant vos in aeterna tabernacula.* *Make you friends of the Mammon of Iniquity, that when you fayle, they may receaue you into eternall Tabernacles.*

FINIS.

God saue the King.